Dear Fr

Dear Friends

The Letters of
St. Paul
to
Christians
in America

Christopher L. Webber

YUCCA

Yucca Publishing books may be purchased in bulk at special discounts for sales promotion, corporate gifts, fund-raising, or educational purposes. Special editions can also be created to specifications. For details, contact the Special Sales Department, Yucca Publishing, 307 West 36th Street, 11th Floor, New York, NY 10018 or yucca@skyhorsepublishing.com.

Yucca Publishing® is an imprint of Skyhorse Publishing, Inc.®, a Delaware corporation.

Visit our website at www.yuccapub.com.

10 9 8 7 6 5 4 3 2 1

Library of Congress Cataloging-in-Publication Data is available on file.

Cover design by Yucca Publishing

Print ISBN: 978-1-63158-015-4
Ebook ISBN: 978-1-63158-025-3

Printed in the United States of America

CONTENTS

INTRODUCTION

THE PURPOSE

Among the most read books of the Bible are the letters written by St. Paul to young churches in Rome and scattered around the eastern end of the Mediterranean Sea. Whether in private reading or in study groups, millions of Christians and even nonbelievers often ask themselves, "What did this mean to those who first read it?" and, "What does this mean for me?"

These are appropriate questions. There is not much purpose in Bible Study that never asks, "What would St. Paul want to say to us now and where we live?" To help people answer that question, scholars have written careful analyses of Paul's letters and provided new translations that seek to provide Paul's words in our own language. Nevertheless these translations and paraphrases continue to give us Paul's opinion on issues of importance to first century Christians and these are not always the same as the issues that concern us.

Many who have studied St. Paul's letters believe that not all of them were written by Paul himself but by followers who set out to provide the letters Paul might have written to the next generation of Christians. The Letter to the Ephesians, for example, is thought by many to have been written after Paul's death as a sort of summary of his teaching for a new generation of Christians. It seems odd, then, that the practice of writing in the spirit of Paul has been allowed to lapse for so long and that no one apparently has attempted to write the letters to today's churches that Paul might write if he were still with us. Paul wrote particular letters

of teaching and advice to particular churches seeking to meet
the needs of particular Christians in Rome and Corinth, Galatia
and Philippi. What letters would he write now to Christians in
Washington and San Francisco, Dallas and Des Moines?

No one, of course, can answer that question with complete
confidence, but Christians in Washington and San Francisco,
Dallas and Des Moines, and many other places large and small, do
attempt to read Paul's letters and provide answers for themselves
daily to guide their lives today. It should not be difficult to put
some of these tentative answers in the form of a letter that could
be read and discussed by others.

This collection of letters, then, simply continues a very old
tradition. These letters can hardly provide definitive answers but
they can make suggestions and provide opportunity for others
to react and to think for themselves about where they agree and
where they might differ. Undoubtedly there will be disagreements,
probably sharp disagreements, as there would be in any Bible study
group but it is only by listening to others who see things differently
that we can test our own understanding and gain new insight into
the ways we can grow in faith.

In writing these new letters, I have tried to listen carefully to
what St. Paul was saying and to study as well what others have
understood him to say and, on that basis to write the letters I think
he would write now. I cannot be sure Paul himself would always
agree with what I have written but Paul was attempting to speak
for Jesus and was not always sure Jesus would have agreed with
him either. He wrote at least once, "I *think* I have the mind of
Christ," but he seems to have been well aware that an element of
uncertainty might remain. Likewise here, I have tried to enter into
the mind of Paul, even though no one can do that with complete
assurance. Inevitably we bring to such an effort our own prejudices,
training, experience, and consequent understanding of the faith.

We may not be sure, but we must get the best guidance we can, pray about it with an open mind, and then move forward—still recognizing that we may be in error and always knowing our need of forgiveness.

These, then, are letters Paul might write to the churches today. They are offered to the churches and individuals for study in confidence that those who study these letters with open minds and prayerful hearts can grow in understanding and make a better witness to others as a result.

THE PLAN

Rome and Corinth and Ephesus and the other cities to which Paul wrote are, obviously, not at all like the cities of modern America, nor are they even like modern Rome and Corinth. Ephesus, once the second largest city in the Roman Empire, exists now only as ruins for tourists to gaze at. Christians in modern America live in very different circumstances. They are not a new, small, somewhat exotic group often considered subversive and even dangerous and sometimes persecuted. Nevertheless Paul did write about matters that concern us still, most especially sex and money and power. It is hard to imagine that his attitude toward promiscuity, wealth, and greed would have changed at all but the fundamental principles he seeks to apply may need to be applied differently in our circumstances. Paul also dealt with matters that were clearly conditioned by culture such as headcoverings for women and meat sacrificed to idols. Here, too, however, his judgments are based on fundamental principles that may have a bearing on issues peculiar to our world. In reading Paul, then, we need always to look for the underlying and unchanging principles and try to apply them to our own time and culture.

To make all this as relevant as possible for contemporary American Christians, it seemed best to try to re-write Paul's letters for specific communities. Rome's nearest equivalent is obviously Washington, both cities being power centers with influence extending throughout their world. After that, matchmaking is more difficult. California may be most like Corinth with its diverse populations and constant seeking for change. Texas, likewise, may have some affinity for Galatia with it's reluctance to let go of the security of laws which may or may not still apply. The Letter to the Ephesians is often said to have been written by a disciple of Paul, possibly the former slave, Onesimus, who apparently became bishop of Ephesus, and might have written it as an introduction to a collection he made of Paul's letters. Certainly it seems better organized than the others and more comprehensive. As such, it seemed best to rewrite it as a general letter to Americans and something of an introduction to the other letters. For that reason, we have moved it to an introductory position rather than leave it in its familiar place which was determined simply by the length of the letters, putting the longest first and the shortest last.

Beyond that, relationships are still more difficult and the pairing of Colossians and Colorado, Philippians and Philadelphia, is more a matter of similarity of name than any specific issues. Few of the issues addressed, however, can be matched exclusively with any one community. The Pauline letters we have were collected and preserved, after all, because they were not applicable only to one community but had much to say to most Christians then as now. So, too, it is hoped that there is much here for Christians everywhere to consider. Each letter should be considered as possibly applicable to some Americans in particular but also, more generally, to Christians everywhere.

This is a collection, then, of ten letters corresponding to the New Testament letters to Rome, Corinth (2), Galatia, Ephesus,

Philippi, Colossae, Thessalonica (2), and Philemon. Some, of course, will argue that one or more of these letters was not written by Paul while others believe that he also wrote the letters to Titus and Timothy. No one known to me still thinks he wrote the Epistle to the Hebrews. All that, however, raises questions to be discussed in other books. I think I am following the consensus of contemporary scholarship in stopping with the ten listed.

As to style, any attempt to follow Paul closely will bring into sharp focus the clarity and force with which he wrote. Jokes are often made about Paul's sometimes wandering, lengthy, and complex sentences but, in fact, he is most often quite direct and forceful. The most complex sentences are in Ephesians which, as I said, he may not have written. I have not attempted simply to rephrase the letters as J. B. Phillips and others have done so well. I have attempted to write instead as nearly as possible in Paul's manner while dealing with current issues in ways that Paul might have done if he applied the same principles to them that he used in his earlier letters.

As to content, I have sometimes felt free to change the subject completely although still holding closely to Paul's principles. So, in writing to Washington now rather than Rome then, a democracy rather than an empire, Paul would, I believe, be able to say more about the proper use of power. I have therefore substituted a discussion of power for Paul's discussion of particular sins. The sexual transgressions about which Paul wrote to the Romans were discussed more extensively in Corinthians so I have dealt with them in his letter to the Californians. So, too, in matters of sex, Paul might feel freer now than he would have been in a patriarchal world to apply his basic principle that "in Christ there is neither male nor female."

Cultural issues that Paul dealt with, such as women speaking in church and wearing head covering, are not yet fully resolved. New issues such as birth control, abortion, same sex marriage, and the death penalty have caused enormous controversy in the church and society. How would Paul apply his standards to these issues? I can suggest one way of handling it but obviously many will differ. Can they justify their positions and can we discuss our differences in Christian charity? Certainly we will not resolve these issues unless we face them and discuss them. If this book can contribute to that process, it will be serving its purpose.

Looking closely at Paul's letters, it is striking how much time he spends on personal matters, mentioning specific names and often sending brief messages to specific individuals. It would have been possible, I suppose, to create a parallel world and mention specific individuals either real or imagined but that seemed not very useful. Some individual names are included and the last letter imagines an individual somewhat like the Philemon Paul wrote to on behalf of Onesumus. But, on balance, these letters are probably not as personal as Paul's and that is worth noting.

I have not divided these letters by verses (nor did Paul!) but I have adopted the traditional pattern of chapters and have kept very closely to Paul's letters in length not only of each letter but chapter by chapter as well. That will make it easier to compare, chapter by chapter what Paul said then with what he might want to say now.

IN CONCLUSION

Some, undoubtedly, will reject these readings as an outrageous twisting of Paul's intent. Let me simply repeat that they are offered out of a deep conviction that they are quite consistent with Paul and with a living faith in Christ. I am not attempting to shake anyone's faith but, if possible, to deepen it. I would ask that readers approach these letters with a willingness to reconsider issues and viewpoints previously unexamined. If they come away with their convictions unchanged, I would hope that they will nevertheless understand better that others can differ with them in good faith and on the basis of their own understanding of the Scriptures. I hope that all who think these issues through, seeking the guidance of the Holy Spirit, whatever their conclusions, will find their own faith renewed and deepened.

THE LETTER TO AMERICANS

(EPHESIANS)

Dear Friends in Christ in America,

Distracted as you must be by the great issues of world affairs, economic and political, that are debated and contested in your country, I write to remind you that this world and its affairs are passing away and that we have been placed here to live into the greater reality to which we are called by the Lord Jesus who has made known to us an eternal destiny encompassing not only the nations of this earth but the vast universe itself with worlds beyond our present knowledge. Science has changed your lives beyond imagining in the last century and there are many who believe those changes—political, economic, and environmental—have consequences beyond human control. Indeed, these forces are, as they have always been, beyond human control but God has called us to work together in the power of the Spirit to use the gifts we are given to create a realm of justice, freedom, and peace. You have expended both lives and treasure in the search for an elusive peace based on human power but we are promised a peace beyond the understanding or attainment of politicians and powers, a peace that is not simply cessation of strife and conflict, but the fulfillment of all our dreams and potential, a joy that never fades away. That peace is based not on human power but on the power of God. May this peace and grace be yours in the Lord Jesus.

I do not, however, write off this present world as a sphere of no importance, as if the certain fulfillment of a future hope absolves us of any concern for the present. It is that very promise of future joy that impels us to work more earnestly for peace and justice in this present age since we know God's will for us and are assured that we are called to be agents of that will. The same Lord Jesus who died for us taught us to pray for the coming of God's reign of righteousness, and what we pray for we must also work for, and what we work for under God's guidance we work for in sure and certain hope of fulfillment. God's will for us is justice and peace. We see and taste that promise even in the present time.

Among those who built your country were many who sought to live out the gospel in freedom and who toiled and sacrificed for the sake of their vision. So successful have they been that your country has drawn many of other faiths and some without faith who sought the freedom and opportunity for which you became known. Indeed, there are many who strive for that vision who know not the Lord who nevertheless works within them and inspires them, for the Spirit is at work in every place and in all people to accomplish God's purpose in creation.

Since, then, your nation has drawn so many who do not share your faith and since your nation is spoken of throughout the world, you have been given an opportunity to hold up the light of the gospel both at home and abroad for the benefit of those who do not know the Lord Jesus. If you are faithful to that gospel and make it known through lives dedicated to peace and justice and if you dedicate yourselves also to listening to others and recognizing the work of the Spirit in their own heritage of faith, you will be effective witnesses to the Lord Jesus. Christ is the end toward whom all faiths must come but we must be ready to see and learn from those of other faiths what the Spirit has done among them that can enrich our own understanding of God. All this is a part of the plan which God has been working out from the first dawn of creation and which has now been revealed to us who acknowledge Jesus as Lord.

I give God thanks and praise for your presence and witness in the varied communities of your society. God chose you for this purpose before the universe came into being and called you to be holy and faithful, to be adopted as children of God through Jesus Christ, and to offer up praise and thanksgiving for the gifts so freely poured out upon us. That purpose can be seen in you who witness to your faith in your daily lives. I pray that you will continue to grow in grace so that the power of the gospel will be evident among you and in the church which is the body of Christ in whom we find the life that God has promised.

2

Consider the nature of the gift you have received as members of the church of Christ, living as you do in a society that has been shaped in many ways by the gospel and by the servants of Christ but that remains divided by fear of the other, the unknown, and the unfamiliar. The fundamental ideals of freedom and justice which all your fellow citizens acknowledge are principles derived from the prophets and taught to us in the gospel as God's will for all people. Many, indeed, honor these principles with their lips while ignoring them in their lives so you must constantly hold them up as followers of Christ, following them yourselves and calling on others to accept and honor them as well. Yet acknowledgment and even acceptance fall short of our calling which is to be the body of Christ in this world so that Christ is seen in us and the principles we accept are made visible as a living reality.

That reality is not a matter of mere individual morality or even personal holiness but of a society incorporated into Christ, redeemed by Christ in you, and transformed into his likeness. There are many who are satisfied with something less, who live faithful lives as individuals without discerning the body. Such witness is too limited. Your nation, like every earthly society, must be transformed by a vision of justice and that requires a ceaseless battle against those who covet wealth and power for themselves while ignoring the needs of others. If you are a society that fails to care for the poorest and neediest among you, the light of the gospel is darkened and others both within your nation and abroad will turn away from a gospel that speaks of love but fails to make it known.

It is to empower us to serve God's purpose in the world and especially among those in need that we have been saved from our sins by grace and raised to a new life in Christ. Apart from Christ we are as good as dead, but in him we have been raised to eternal life. This is not our doing; it is by God's grace that we are saved and our faith is always simply a response to God's initiative. In proclaiming the gospel to others, we must remember that we have no more natural right to salvation than they; we are all alike inheritors of a human nature alienated from God and incapable of returning to unity with God and each other by our own activity. It is by virtue of the cross and the blood of Christ that we who were estranged from God are brought near. It is his death and resurrection that breaks down the walls of division we erect out of fear of each other and it is his resurrection that brings life to all and unites the divided families of the earth. It is his gift of life that you bring to your society with the promise that those divided in ethnic communities and separated by language and history and every human prejudice can become a new community in Christ. He is our peace and the hope of the world's peace.

3

Remember the commission I was given at the beginning to carry the gospel of life to the nations of the world and how God's eternal purpose was revealed to me: that the nations should be given a share in the riches of Christ and become heirs of the promise together with us and members of the same body. I was the least deserving of all the people of Israel, yet God commanded me to carry this message to the nations and make known to them the wisdom of

God in all its richness and power so that all people might see the mystery which was hidden in former times but is now revealed to his servants by the Spirit and is to be made known through the church in all its rich variety, not only to those holding power in governments and other institutions, to the wise and educated, but to the poorest and most forsaken and ignorant as well, for it is God's good pleasure to unite all people in Christ Jesus our Lord. It is in him that we have access to God and are able to approach the throne of grace in boldness and confidence.

Do not lose heart or abandon this hope that we are given. There must be times of hardship and testing without which faith will not come to its full growth. It is for your sake that I have endured much suffering and for your sake that I bend my knee in prayer to our Creator, the One who gave birth to us as a mother gives birth to a child, and who has given us a name as parents name their children so that we may be called the children of God and heirs of God in Christ Jesus.

My prayer for you is that you will not be satisfied with simple answers, rejecting all that is to be learned from biologists and environmentalists of the intricate and beautiful texture of creation and failing to accept the challenge of working with God to preserve and enhance what the heedless and arrogant would destroy, but that growing in wisdom and understanding you will unite faith and reason for the benefit of all. May you sink your roots deeply in the knowledge of Christ so that in him, with all God's saints, you will be empowered to glimpse the height and depth and length and breadth of that love which sustains the universe and which remains beyond the reach of human understanding. May the power of God at work within us accomplish more than we can either ask or imagine; to God be glory in the church and in Christ Jesus to all generations, forever and ever. Amen.

4

Since all this is true, I beg you fervently to lead lives that really reflect our knowledge of the glory of God. You cannot do that in anger or arrogance or by quarreling among yourselves. You must make every effort possible with the guidance and grace of God's Spirit within you to live in unity and peace. In spite of the tragic history of Christian divisions, there can be only one body as there is only one Spirit and one hope held out to you; there is only one Lord, one faith, one baptism, and one God who gave us birth and who reigns above us, works within us, and calls us to be one.

Within that essential unity, each of us is given particular gifts for our ministry and each of us has a ministry to carry out which cannot be delegated to others. These ministries are a gift to us out of the abundance of Christ's blessing. He came among us so that he could give us gifts and returned to his place at the center of the universe so that he might now be present in each of us and in all creation. Those gifts he gives us are many and varied; there are preachers and teachers and bishops and pastors and priests and musicians and missionaries whose work is to enable God's chosen people to do the work of ministry in the world and to build up the church, the body of Christ, until we all come together at last in such unity of faith and knowledge of Jesus that we can measure up at last to Christ himself.

We cannot do this and act like children, quarreling over every detail of faith and life. The world around us is delighted to see us act that way and will be quick to publicize our failures, indeed they will encourage us to display our differences and help us create new divisions. Especially when we attempt to use the law to accomplish our goals do we play into the hands of Satan. We have work enough to regulate our own lives without seeking to govern others. The path Jesus followed was one of humility and patience, forbearance and suffering; never compulsion and power. So we must come to that maturity that has no need of praise or pride and thus play our proper part in the life of the whole body, with every bone and sinew working together in love and selflessness for the good of the whole.

Let me tell you as clearly as I can that we must not live like those around us whose lives are centered on sports, entertainment, and self-indulgence, who have no concern for eternal values or even their neighbor's need. This is not what you learned about Jesus! I know you have heard the gospel and been taught the basics of faith and that you were instructed to put off a way of life centered on self so that you can make room for the Spirit and put on your new self, remodeled in the likeness and image of God in true righteousness and holiness. So live that way, and deal with your neighbors with integrity for we are members of one body. Simple things make a difference: if you are angry, get over it before the day is over; make no room in your life for Satan.

Do not be seduced by false values. Money is a false god; do not give your life to pursuing it, especially by deceiving others, and put aside some of what you earn to share with others. Speak honestly and truthfully so your words will create unity and not division. Put away all anger and discord and argumentativeness and maliciousness. Be kind to other people, and forgive each other, remembering that God in Christ has first forgiven you.

5

Act toward others as God acts toward you and imitate God as children imitate their parents. Make love your priority because Christ loved us and gave himself up for us as a beautiful offering to God. Never let greed or any kind of sexual misbehavior even be mentioned among you; why would saints have their minds in the gutter? Obscenity and vulgarity and blasphemous use of God's holy Name have no place in your mouths; you have the gift of speech in order to express your love for each other and to give praise to God. You can be sure that no one who exploits others through sexual misbehavior or greed for wealth has any hope of eternal life with Christ and with God. Don't let people fool you or tell you such things don't matter. It is this kind of behavior that destroys human relationships and corrupts society. Don't be corrupted by those around you but do not isolate yourselves from them either. You must be a light to a society that is losing its way; live as children of the light undaunted by the darkness around you but exposing the evils you see and drawing others to the light. Let the Easter light of the risen Christ be visible in your lives throughout the year and sing out your joy in psalms and hymns, giving thanks at all times to God and in all things to our risen Lord.

Seek for Christ in each other and serve one another as you would serve Christ. Partners in marriage in particular should serve each other, putting the other's needs and interests ahead of their own. You should love each other as Christ loves the church and gave his life for its members to create a holy and unblemished body, washed and purified by the baptism of faith so that it might be united with him in splendor in the great marriage feast to which we are summoned. Marriage is a holy vocation through which the partners learn to submit themselves to each other in joyful obedience so that their marriage becomes a school of heaven and a foretaste of eternal joy. To love another in marriage is to love yourself for you become one flesh and care for the other as you would care for yourself and as Christ also cares for you. This uniting of two human beings in faithful and enduring relationships is a great mystery since it calls us beyond the merely physical life of the body to experience the deeper unity surpassing human understanding to which we are called by God's great love for us. It is in the deepest physical unity that the fullest spiritual unity is discovered for God has created us with bodies that speak most eloquently of those invisible spiritual gifts through which alone the fullest meaning of life is realized. Let your love for each other reflect God's love for you and deepen your love for God.

6

Parents should teach their children the value of self-control so that the human family becomes a model of the church, controlled by love and concern first for the other. Be gentle with each other and seek occasions to be together at meals and in times of leisure. Be patient when times of conflict come and, when there is disagreement, listen carefully to what others are saying. Find your joy in seeking each other's happiness. Above all, center your lives in worship and prayer so that you find the strength and guidance that God alone can give.

In your places of work and in your community also seek first of all to serve. Anger and impatience serve only to create ill will and deepen divisions, but your calling is to work for unity and understanding in the common tasks we are given. Work with enthusiasm for the welfare of others and draw others into the work for many discover the meaning and joy of faith through community service. Serve the needs of others as you would serve the Lord and remember that the Lord will serve and strengthen you in all things.

One last word of advice: find your strength in the Lord and the power of the Spirit. Think of yourselves as athletes in training for a spiritual contest so that you may be able to withstand the temptations and opposition that will come. For our struggle is not simply against opponents of flesh and blood but against the very real cosmic powers of darkness and the spiritual forces of evil that surround us day by day. So put yourself in training and take on the discipline required to excel in any activity. As an athlete finds

time to exercise and takes on a diet that will provide nourishment
for the whole body, so you must set aside regular times for prayer
and for meditating on the word of God and for sharing the bread
of life at the Lord's table. As an athlete needs a trainer, so you must
seek the spiritual counsel of a wise advisor who can share with
you the experience gained through years of practice. Set high goals
and work patiently toward them without allowing yourself to be
distracted by those without discipline. Rely on the Word of God
for guidance and reassurance and let your whole life become an
offering of prayer. Pray also for me that I may continue to be able
to bear witness boldly to the gospel, that message of grace that is
more than any words can express.

I will continue to send personal messengers to you to encourage
you with their witness as well as my words. You are all very dear
to me and your faithfulness is especially critical at this time. May
peace and love from God and the Lord Jesus Christ fill your hearts
and minds. Grace be to all who have an undying love for Jesus our
Lord and Savior.

THE LETTER TO WASHINGTON

(ROMANS)

Dear Friends in Washington,

As you may know, I have been called by Jesus Christ to be his ambassador and commissioned to proclaim to the whole world the good news of God's love and power. The news I proclaim is the truth that was first announced by the prophets and was then made clear to everyone by the life, death, and resurrection of Jesus Christ. I have obeyed my calling by traveling throughout the world and working night and day to strengthen God's people and build up the church of Christ.

For many years, it has been my hope that I could also visit those of you who live in the great city of Washington so that I could share with you in the vital work of witness that you are carrying out. Everywhere in the world people talk about your commitment to the Christian faith so I would like to take counsel with you about your witness. I hope God will enable me to come to you before much longer but meanwhile this letter will assure you of my concern for your welfare.

It has been my privilege over the years to share the work of the gospel with people of every race and nation and I have been greatly enriched by this experience. I think I have gained a deeper understanding of the various ways in which people hear the gospel—or fail to hear it—and I have seen how it is that sometimes the witness we bear may be ineffective because we are misunderstood. This is why I really hope to visit you at last and be renewed in the Spirit by the mutual sharing of God's grace. Meanwhile I give thanks for your obedience to God and your fellowship in the gospel.

I want you to know that everywhere in the world God's servants look to you and hold you in their prayers. They know how vital it is that you be unequaled in your witness since so many others think of you, for better or worse, as the clearest examples of the meaning of Christian faith. Your faithful witness brings glory to the gospel but your failures create confusion for Christians everywhere. That is why we pray that you will have gifts of grace and strength to resist the temptations of worldly power. You know that such power is a snare of the evil one and that those who seek it bring destruction upon themselves and many others.

Greed and the lust for power always draw men and women away from the service of God. All people are subject to its corruption even though God has made it plain that those who seek for selfish gain have turned away from the light and walk in darkness, far from the purpose for which they were created. It is because of this that wars and conflicts still trouble all the earth and lead to every kind of suffering and misery, and these are so evident that those who continue on in their greed, blind to the suffering they cause, have no excuse for their wickedness.

"Do you," I would ask such people, "imagine that God is unaware of your disobedience? Do you suppose that the God who has given life and breath to human beings everywhere is indifferent to the evil that you do? When you study God's word, do you not hear what that word says?" Scripture says that the love of money is the root of all evil. Placed as you are in the midst of so much wealth, you must take special care to avoid its temptation. There are many around you who will offer you great wealth if you will represent their interests. You must pray constantly for strength to resist such temptations.

Not everyone, of course, is a follower of Jesus and has come to a clearer understanding of God's will for human life, but every human being can see the justice and mercy of the Creator. Everything human beings can know of God is obvious in all creation. God sends down rain on the just and the unjust alike and God's hand is open to feed all living creatures. So when anyone heaps up riches and ignores the needs of others, that person has no excuse for what they have done. People like that have traded the truth of God for a lie and worship the created thing rather than the Creator who is blessed for ever. Amen.

It is because such people have wandered so far from the truth that God has given them up to their idolatry and their corrupt imaginations so that they go blindly on their way indulging themselves in all the luxuries of life while others, even children, suffer needlessly and die. These people are shameless in the extravagance of their ways, building great mansions for themselves while others are homeless and eating the most expensive luxury foods while others go hungry. Meanwhile, those who are chosen as leaders use their positions not to serve human need but to satisfy their own desire for power and wealth. They are so consumed by their greed that they practice every kind of wickedness, evil, gluttony, deceit, and malice. They imagine themselves to be honorable people and they are honored by many, but in fact they are filled with envy, murder, and craftiness; they are slanderers, insolent, haughty, boastful, foolish, faithless, heartless, ruthless. It is obvious to everyone that those who do such things do not deserve to live, yet they continue in their rebelliousness and encourage others to follow their evil example.

2

So you have no excuse, whoever you are, if you condemn others for their moral failures while you yourself fall short in other ways. In condemning them, you condemn yourself, because you yourself, when you presume to judge your neighbor, are equally guilty. You point at others and say, "We know that God condemns behavior like that." But when God calls us to holiness, we are not only called to personal piety but also to care for our neighbors in their need. Do you imagine, when you judge others for their personal weaknesses that you yourself, who show no concern for others, can escape judgment? Do you imagine that the patience and mercy of God have no limits? Do you not understand that God is patient only to allow you time for repentance? If, then, you continue to misuse God's gifts, you can be certain that God will deal with you according to your behavior. God will judge all people according to what they have done. Those who have persisted in seeking to serve others according to the gifts they have been given, whether they are Christians, Jews, or Muslims, will find the doorway open to eternal life, while those who seek only their own advantage, whoever they are, will inherit anguish and distress.

All human beings fall short of God's will and God shows no partiality in judging. Those who have heard the good news will be judged according to the knowledge they have been given, while those who have not heard the gospel proclaimed will be judged according to the truth they have found apart from the gospel, for all human beings have received some understanding of God's will. We should never imagine that it is only those who have heard the gospel and call themselves Christians who are righteous in God's sight; it is all those who do what God requires. When non-Christians who have not heard the gospel do instinctively what the gospel requires, they make it clear that the gospel is written on their hearts and that they are obedient to their consciences, formed by God's Spirit at work within them. Their own consciences therefore will judge them for good or ill in that day when God will act through Jesus Christ to make known the secrets of every heart and call into judgement the peoples of the world.

If you call yourself a Christian and claim to be born again and talk publicly about your relationship with God and how you take part in Bible study and believe in everything written in God's word and consider yourself an excellent example of Christian living, and if you teach Sunday school and serve on church committees, shouldn't you also teach yourself? If you condemn stealing, do you then steal from others by manipulating corporate accounts? If you condemn adultery, do you lure others into sexual sin by sexually explicit advertising? You that condemn the worship of false gods, do you make a god out of your material possessions? You are so proud of being a Christian, yet you dishonor the name of Christ by your actions. No wonder Scripture says, God's followers are constantly criticized by others.

Being born again is certainly a good thing, if you truly seek God's will; but if you seek only your own convenience, your new birth becomes a second death. And if those who do not think of themselves as born again truly seek God's will, will not their seeking be counted as new birth? So those who are not Christians but provide for the needs of others and work for peace are right to condemn you who behave outwardly like a Christian but do nothing to serve human need. A Christian is not simply someone who goes to church on Sunday; being born again is a matter of the heart—it is spiritual, but it transforms the whole person. People who are transformed in that way may not win praise from others, but God will certainly honor them at the last.

3

So what advantage is there in being a Christian? What is the point of being born again? Why would you even ask? The knowledge of the gospel of Jesus Christ is beyond all price. We have been given this great gift and even if some are unfaithful, God's gift remains of value beyond all measure. Does the fact that some are faithless mean that God is not faithful? Of course not! Even if every human being proved false, God would still be faithful. The Bible says God's word will always turn out to be true, no matter who denies it.

There are some who like to emphasize human sinfulness to make God's goodness look even better. But if our sinfulness makes God look good, does that mean our sinfulness serves a good purpose and it would be unfair of God to condemn us? Would it even be possible to suggest—as some say I have done—that we should commit even greater sins so that God's goodness may be made even more clear? No; absolutely not! That's a terrible distortion.

But it is certainly true in one sense that we have no advantage over others. We have already shown that all human beings are under the power of sin. The Bible says, There is no one who is righteous; not even one. There is no one with any understanding, no one who truly seeks God. No human being has a right to expect God's love, not even someone who has acted faithfully and lovingly toward God or toward others. All human beings, in God's sight, are as good as dead. They use their mouths to curse and their feet to turn to evil. They cause only destruction and sorrow. They know nothing about peace at all. They have no concern for God's will.

Now it is obvious that the Bible is speaking directly to us as Christians precisely to keep us from thinking we can claim special privileges. The message of the Bible is that all human beings are in need of the gospel and accountable to God for their behavior. The more clearly we see God's will for us, the more clearly we see our failures. The Bible makes us more aware than ever of our need for God's help.

So it is not the Bible that saves us or any other scripture; that can only show us our failures. It is Jesus himself who reveals God's love fully, but that love is seen in part in every human religion and God makes no distinction among us. All are in need and all can come to a deeper knowledge of God through the death of Jesus Christ. God offered Jesus to us to show God's gracious care and enable us to respond in faith. All past history simply demonstrates God's patience with us. Though we are slow to respond, God continues to offer all human beings the opportunity to respond and come to God in faith.

So what can we boast of? Nothing at all. Can we boast of the Bible? No, not even that, because it is God who saves us when we respond in faith. God is not the God of Christians only. God is at work among Jews and Muslims and everyone who seeks God in truth. All human beings can find God at work in their lives. Christians will be brought to God through their faith and so will Jews and Muslims and others by their faith. Does this make the Bible of no value? No, not at all; on the contrary, it is the teaching of the Bible that I am upholding.

4

The traditional understanding of Scripture is that Abraham is the ancestor of our faith. We should notice, however, that although the Scriptures recognize his faith, that faith was lived out before God had given the Law and before there was any knowledge of Jesus Christ and the gospel. Yet we read that Abraham was acceptable to God because he responded in obedience and acted out of faith in a God who was still only dimly known to him. So we have to believe that God will continue to recognize the faith of those who serve God in a similar way in our own day as well.

Let me ask you now to consider, for example, how faith has been at work in many diverse individuals. In this era, there has been perhaps no greater example of faith than Mahatma Gandhi, but the witness of Christian people was such a scandal that it left him unable to profess Christian faith in any formal way. Yet Gandhi often said that he admired and worshiped Jesus. What then are we to say of such a man? Shall we say that he was not righteous in God's sight? Jesus himself said, "In my Father's house are many dwelling places. If this were not so, I would have told you,"[1] and

Peter, one of the leading Apostles said, "In truth, I see that God shows no partiality. Rather, in every nation whoever fears God and acts uprightly is acceptable to God."[2]

Don't you see, then, that we can be too narrow in our definition of faith and our judgment of those with whom God will be pleased? We understand, of course, that it is not works that justify the individual. It is not at all sufficient simply to be nice to others and lead a helpful life among our family and friends. I am not suggesting that God seeks only good deeds or judges us on that basis. What I am saying is that God seeks those in every nation whose lives are governed by a deep commitment to the highest spiritual values they have discovered, who seek to serve God unselfishly in others and to respond to God's spirit moving them from within.

There are many people in all nations who act out of faith even though they might not use such words. Consider for example, not only Mahatma Gandhi, but also Nelson Mandela, Martin Luther King, Jr., Mother Teresa, Abraham Heschel, Dag Hammarskjold, Simone Weil, and many others who served God in this age. Not all were formally members of the Church of Christ, but all were recognized as people of faith and their faith inspired many others both within the church and beyond it.

This is why I say that we must not define faith too narrowly. We must acknowledge that God is at work in many ways in many people and in many places. We will serve God best in our own day when we make common cause with such people and seek for the spirit of God even where God is not formally named.

5

If then it is faith that brings us into unity with God's purpose, it is that faith that gives us peace through Jesus Christ our Lord. It is he who opens up to us the gifts God pours out on us and the hope of an ever deeper knowledge of God's love transforming our lives. Even when we face times of suffering, we know that God is with us and can use that suffering to deepen us spiritually, since suffering requires endurance and endurance strengthens our character, and hope becomes central to our lives. Hope, in turn, never disappoints us because it teaches us to depend ever more completely on the Holy Spirit poured into our hearts.

Notice how it is that when our need is greatest we are most aware of God's presence, just as it was when the world was most dominated by the human power of the Roman Empire that God came to those who had no power within that society. How else could God demonstrate love for us so effectively? It is when we are sinful that God comes to us, not when we are righteous or self-righteous.

We human beings are just the opposite. We go all out for our friends but don't have much time for our enemies. We try to dominate them rather than let them have their way with us. And even if we begin to understand this in our personal relationships, we don't apply it to our business relationships, political relationships, and international relationships.

You need to understand that what is true in one situation or relationship is true in all. Sin blinds us to our sinfulness and enables us to act in much of our lives in a way that is different from the way God in Christ acted toward us. As a result, we offer our worship and prayer but evil continues to spread. So one sinful act spreads out and corrupts the whole society, but one perfect act of love has spread out to include the whole human race.

Think of Adam as the origin of sin and of Christ as the source of life. We can see how it often takes only one human being to corrupt an institution or a society. That corruption affects us all whether we consent to it or not. But Christ's gift of life is different:

each of us can accept that gift and have a transforming effect on everyone else. We are victims of sin whether we choose it or not because the sin of one corrupts the whole society. On the other hand, when we choose to accept the free gift of grace, that gift brings life to all.

Do you see how this free gift to us of Christ's life and death and resurrection provides the correcting balance the world needs? Human disobedience is overcome by Christ's perfect obedience. The pattern of human behavior that leads only to death is overcome by the new God-given pattern that leads to life. The power of sin to control us is defeated by the grace we are offered in Christ.

6

Now if our sins lead God to pour down such gifts, would it make any sense to continue to sin in order to bring down new showers of blessing? The idea is laughable! How can we call ourselves Christians and continue to ignore God's will? Don't you know that baptism involves sharing Christ's death in order to share his life? We share his death in baptism so that we can really share his risen life right now. The change from the life being lived by others in the world around us and the life that we might have lived if we were not baptized is the change from death to life. One way of life ends completely and a new way of life begins. Do you really understand that? Do you think others around you see that grace at work when they see the way you live?

It is really important that you understand this central fact about Christian living; there can't be any room for compromise or "halfway" Christianity. Politicians always need to compromise and the temptation to compromise our faith is bound to be strong. But think what that says to the rest of the world about the meaning of Christian faith. It makes the gospel seem hypocritical to them and ultimately meaningless. We make claims as Christians but the world sees nothing different. How is that possible if we really understand what the gospel means?

As Christians we have died to the way of life we see around us and opened ourselves to a way that has nothing in common with that old way. We are talking about the difference between death and life. Just as Christ was crucified and died, so our mortal bodies are crucified with him and die with him so that we can live with him now and forever. But this risen life must be completely new and no longer controlled by the priorities of this world. Others may feel compelled to compromise their values for the sake of their careers or their self-interest, but these concerns can have no power over those who truly live in Christ.

You surely know that when you go to work for an employer or a political party, you offer yourself to serve that employer's purpose or that party's agenda. You can't compromise and work sometimes for that employer or that party and sometimes in opposition. No more can you serve a personal agenda sometimes and God sometimes. Before you became Christians, you were servants of sin and were free of obligation to God, but now you have become servants of Christ and are free from the claims of evil purposes. Now you belong to God whose purpose is to make you holy. The compensation for serving sin is death but God's free gift to us is eternal life in Jesus Christ our Lord. Choose life, therefore, and stop compromising with evil.

7

Doesn't everyone know that a contract is valid only so long as the signer of the contract is alive? If you sign an exclusive agreement with an employer and the employer dies, you are free to sign an agreement with someone else. If you sign another agreement while

the first is still in force, you are guilty under the law; but if the
first employer dies, you are free to work for another. That's the
situation you are in simply as a human being. As human beings we
are subject to all the weaknesses of the flesh and fall short of God's
purpose for us in creation and are bound by the laws of nature to
die. As long as we live the ordinary life of human beings, the urges
of the flesh are able to control us and the inevitable result is death.
If, however, you die with Christ, the law of nature loses its hold on
you and you are free from the death we otherwise can never avoid.

The Bible sums up these failures of human nature in a written
law for our guidance but it does nothing to overcome our
weakness. Is it possible, then, to say that the Bible is sin? No, of
course not. All the Bible really does is show us what we ought to be
and the hopelessness of our situation, and that is what we need to
know. If there were no written law, I would at least not know the
hopelessness of my situation but when I study the Bible I find that
law written down and am clearly shown what sort of person I am.
If I had not read the command, "You shall not covet," I would not
be so aware of my constant coveting. I could be content with my
life if I had never read the Bible, but when I read it I find myself
condemned.

I know the Bible is good, but how can what is good condemn
me to death? Can the good Bible lead me to the pathway of death?
No, not at all! What happens is that the Bible simply reveals what I
might not otherwise see and makes me aware of my need for help.

When I think about the way I act, I can't understand why I do
what I do. I know perfectly well what I ought to be doing, but
somehow I fail to do it. Now if I know what I ought to do but
fail to do it, I agree that the law is good. When I fail to keep it, it
seems to me that it isn't really I that act wrongly but that there is
some power deep within me that is acting against my own will and
against the law. I can will to do right but my will is defeated by

some inner power. What an unhappy man I am! Who can rescue me from this dreadful power within? Thanks be to God, Jesus Christ has already given me victory. My human will, serving my body's desires, remains enslaved by sin but my heart is given to Christ.

8

The good news is that those who belong to Christ Jesus are no longer condemned to death. God has done what the Law could not do because it relied on human beings who were weakened by sin. What God did, therefore, was to come into our human life in the person of Jesus Christ to live under the Law and accept in that human body the consequences of our disobedience. There was no way we could have done this for ourselves. Human nature, corrupted by sin, is too weak to do what is necessary.

Year after year, human beings have held up lofty ideals and worked to transform human society, but the noblest ideals and idealists always fall short. The weight that holds us down is too heavy for ordinary human beings to lift; we cannot overcome the power that overcame us in the first place. God has acted therefore to do for us what we could not do for ourselves, but he has done it in a human body so that we could share in the victory that has been won on our behalf. When we are united with Christ by the power of the Spirit, it becomes possible for us to be empowered by that same Spirit and act no longer under the control of the body's desires and limited by its weakness but to act by the power of the Spirit. To live under the control of the human body's desires is death, but to live in the power of the Spirit is life and peace.

So then, my friends, those who let themselves be controlled by human appetites and goals cannot obey the Law of God; they are living with their minds closed to the will of God, disregarding

God's law, and therefore unable to please God. But you are not governed by that mentality because you have opened your life to the power of the Spirit. Those whose lives are empowered by the Spirit belong to God. Death continues to work in them through the power of sin in their human bodies, but the Spirit of God is working in them to renew them and give them life. If that same Spirit that was able to raise Jesus from death lives in you, that Spirit will give life to your human body also.

We are not obligated, my friends, to live as others live. To live that way is death. But if by the Spirit's power we put the instincts of the mortal body to death, then we will begin to live. And everyone who is led by the Spirit of God is a child of God and leads a transformed life. We no longer live in fear of others because our primary allegiance is not to human standards. The fact that we cry out to God as "Father" is evidence that the Spirit within us is joined with the Spirit of God and that we are indeed God's children. If we are God's children, we are also heirs of God just as Jesus is. If, then, we are indeed children of God and share Christ's inheritance of the heavenly realm and are to be glorified with him, we must also, of course, share in his sufferings. But whatever sufferings we endure now are insignificant when compared to the glory that is our destiny. Our destiny is bound up with that of this whole incredible universe. We are only beginning to understand how completely interdependent our lives are with that not only of the earthly environment but of the seemingly infinite cosmos. God has placed us here as stewards of all creation and all creation awaits our fulfillment to find its own completion and perfection. The present agonies of human life are no cause for despair; we wait with patient hope for the future and see the present turmoil as the birth pangs of the new creation, and the joy we have as members of Christ is a first taste of the banquet to which we are invited.

Even now, while we wait, when words fail us and our prayers are inadequate, we are strengthened and guided by the Spirit within us. And God who knows all things understands the wordless prayers of that Spirit who prays on our behalf.

How wonderful it is that from the very beginning God has chosen us and called us to participate in God's purpose for all creation, and those God has chosen and called will participate in Christ's glory. What else needs to be said? If God is with us, what is there to fear? Who can bring any valid charge against us? It is God who is the final judge. Who could condemn us? No one except Christ, but it is Christ who died for us and was raised for us and stands before God as our advocate. Who can separate us from love like that? Can hardship or distress or sickness, earthquake, fire, or flood? Scripture says, "Because of you we are being killed all day long, and accounted as sheep for the slaughter."[3] But in all such things we are more than triumphant through the Lord who loves us. I am convinced that neither death nor life, nor human authority, nor spiritual powers, nor present difficulties, nor future dangers, nor anything else in all creation can separate us from the love of God in Jesus Christ our Lord.

9

Nothing causes me such pain, my friends, as the divisions among the children of Abraham. I could almost wish that I were cut off from Christ if these brothers and sisters of mine who call themselves Jews and Christians and Muslims could be brought together to serve our merciful God. These are my own flesh and blood and God has called them to a common purpose. It is the Jewish people to whom the promise was first made and God is faithful; those to whom the promise was made will not be forsaken. Does not the Scripture foresee a day when people from nations of every language shall take hold of a Jew, grasping his garment and saying, "Let us go with you, for we have heard that God is with you,"[4] and again Scripture says, "I will bring them to my holy mountain, and make them joyful in my house of prayer; their burnt offerings and their sacrifices will be accepted on my altar; for my house shall be called a house of prayer for all peoples."[5]

So then God has set the Jewish people at the center of the plan of salvation but that plan includes all the world's people, for again Scripture says that: "from the rising of the sun to its setting, the name of the Lord is to be praised."[6] Why then are we at war with each other? Why is it that we consider only the differences among us and ignore what we have in common? Scripture asks:

"Have we not all one father? Has not one God created us? Why then are we faithless to one another, profaning the covenant of our ancestors?"[7]

Yet God has set before us the vision of a day when:
the mountain of the LORD's house
shall be established as the highest of the mountains,
and shall be raised above the hills.
Many peoples shall come and say:
"Come, let us go up to the mountain of the LORD,
to the house of the God of Jacob;
that he may teach us his ways and that we may walk in his paths."
For out of Zion shall go forth instruction,
and the word of the LORD from Jerusalem.[8]
Then will come also the day we long for when:
they shall beat their swords into plowshares,
and their spears into pruning hooks;
nation shall not lift up sword against nation,
neither shall they learn war any more.[9]

If this, then, is the vision God sets before us, why is that we still rely on weapons and military strength? Did not the prophet Isaiah condemn such failure to rely on God and tell you:

> Thus said the Lord GOD, the Holy One of Israel:
> In returning and rest you shall be saved;
> in quietness and in trust shall be your strength."[10]
> But you have refused and said,
> "No, we will have strong weapons!
> Therefore your enemies also have strong weapons
> and God's Name is blasphemed
> even by those who call themselves a righteous people.

You say quite rightly that God's will for all people is freedom and justice and peace but how are you free when you burden yourselves with the cost of war and how is peace created by endless conflict and how is it that you would make yourselves the arbiters of justice? Do you truly believe that God's will can only be done by a nation that has superior power? So also the Romans believed but their power did not save them. So also in the day of Christendom those with power sought to establish God's will through human law but the churches they established relied on human power and made themselves resented and at last irrelevant.

Yet God continues to work secretly and asks us to wait patiently for God's purpose to be revealed. You are always in a hurry and are quick to see opposition where God's ways are hidden from you. Do you not remember that:

> the LORD waits to be gracious to you;
> For the LORD is a God of justice;
> blessed are all those who wait for him.[11]

So then we must wait in confidence knowing that God is able to do far more than we either desire or deserve and can work even through those who appear to be God's enemies turning even persecutors into instruments of God's will, for it depends not on human will or exertion but on God who shows mercy.

What if God, in order to make known God's power, has waited patiently for you to recognize your inability to shape history according to your vision and used even those who seem to be God's enemies to accomplish that purpose? Who are we to complain that we have built great churches and made long prayers if at last we have trusted in what we have built for ourselves and not a Creator whose ways may be hidden from us? God has always sought out the humble and rejected those who pile up treasure for themselves.

10

Dear friends, my heart's desire and daily prayer to God is that the church I have labored to build may be saved. I know full well the zeal with which you seek to serve God but I see also that it is not always enlightened by a willingness to admit your ignorance of God's purpose and is often frustrated by a false confidence in your understanding of God's will. How often God has found it necessary to humble those who have been called! So the Scripture says to God's chosen,

I will make you jealous with what is no people;
provoke them with a foolish nation.[12]

Isaiah goes so far as to say,

I was ready to be sought out by those who did not ask;

to be found by those who did not seek me.[13]

But of the church he says,

All day long I have held out my hands
to a disobedient and contrary people.[14]

So then we find that God is able to work through all those who
seek God, even those who oppose God's will. But where there
is a living faith in the one God who made all people and calls
them into obedience we can be yet more confident of what can be
accomplished, for the scripture says, "No one who believes in God
will be put to shame."[15] There is no distinction made between Jew
and Christian and Muslim, for the same Lord is Lord of all and is
generous to all who call on him. For, "Everyone who calls on the
name of the Lord shall be saved."[16]

Is there then no need to call on the name of Jesus? Yes, but that
name is pronounced in many ways by those who love him and
there are many who call on him by other names as well. There are
also some who hold him to be only one of the prophets and so do
not understand that in him dwelt all the fulness of God. But shall
we allow our narrow perceptions to be the final arbiters of truth
and require perfect agreement before we reach out to our brothers
and sisters? Is our faith so full and final that we can make no room
for others on the road?

I wish you all could understand the gospel with the fulness and
clarity that I have been given, but not all are called to be teachers
and evangelists, not all have had opportunity to give many hours
and years to deepen their faith; not all, even among the apostles,
were or are in perfect agreement as to Christ's saving work. But
faith need not wait for perfect understanding nor does love need
to wait for perfection in faith. It is surely less important to seek out

differences than to seek out those things that unite us, for God is
a God of unity, not division, and to serve God need not wait until
all can use the same words with the same understanding.

But how will others call on God in Christ Jesus if they cannot
see the Spirit at work in us and how will they see the Spirit in us if
they see no evidence of unity and how will we be united unless we
put aside the things that divide?

11

I ask then, Has God rejected God's people? By no means!
Although the greater part of Israel has not acknowledged Christ,
they have remained faithful to their call through great suffering and
persecution and God who called them first is faithful. Likewise the
church, though often divided and distracted by controversy, still
proclaims the name of Jesus and is able to make new disciples and
to transform lives. But consider how, when the church grew cold a
new witness to the one God who made us arose in Islam and with
new zeal reached out to those who had not heard the gospel and
drew many nations to submit to the faith of Abraham. It is true
that they do not acknowledge Jesus as Lord or bear witness to the
resurrection, but they proclaim one God and demand obedience to
God and charity to God's people. See then how the failure of some
has meant life for others and how God has used the church's failure
to bring many from pagan darkness into a fuller light.

So, as in former times Israel's stumbling meant riches for the
Gentiles, now also the church's stumbling has meant wealth for
distant nations and tribes. If then the stumbling of God's chosen
has meant riches for others, think how much wealth their final
unity will bring. I am speaking to you who are Christians since I
was made an apostle to the new Israel but I point to God's work
in Islam to make you jealous and renew your faith, for if your

weakness has meant light for others, what will the final unity of God's people mean except life from the dead!

Even if a tree has many branches, life flows to them all from the same root and if the root is holy, then the branches also are holy, and if you, who were not called at first are now numbered along the chosen, why should you be surprised to find that others also are called? It may be that the other branches produce less abundant fruit at the moment but you must remember that whatever fruit you produce comes from the richness of the root and is not your work. It is through faith that you are able to produce fruit to the glory of God and not by your own efforts. Remember also that the gardener will prune some branches for the benefit of the others and even cut some off so that others may be grafted in. There is therefore no room for pride; the branch that is favored today may be cut off and discarded tomorrow. It is through God's grace alone that you are able to bear fruit to the glory of God. Notice also that the gardener is able to shape the tree according to his plan; it is not for the branches to question that design but only to give thanks if they are counted as useful to serve God's purpose for a time.

You may say that we are saved by faith alone through grace; that is true, but God is able to have mercy on those to whom God will show mercy. Just as Abraham was saved through obedience before faith was revealed, so also many may be saved now by their obedience who do not know the full gospel of God.

I want you to understand this mystery, my friends: God is able to raise up children to Abraham from the stones, but it is God's loving purpose to draw those who are called into the kingdom, and it is first through those who acknowledge Abraham as their ancestor that God is revealed to the whole world. Does not the Scripture also bear witness that in God's good time

All kings shall bow down before him;
All nations shall come to serve him.[17]

How deep and beyond all knowing are the riches and wisdom
and knowledge of God! How unsearchable are his judgments and
how inscrutable his ways! For "to the Lord every knee shall bow"[18]
and "who has directed the Spirit of the Lord"[19] for to the Lord be
ascribed all honor, power, and dominion, now and forever. Amen.

12

I appeal to you, brothers and sisters, by the mercies of God to
offer your living bodies as a sacrifice, withholding nothing of all
that God has given you from the work of the gospel. To offer to
God the material gifts we are given is a vital part of our spiritual
worship. The whole world belongs to its Creator and is given us
to enjoy, but it is our ministry to renew and transform the world
by our faithfulness and not let the enjoyment of worldly things
separate us from God.

Through the grace that God has given me, I call on you not to
let positions of power and influence in church or state lead you to
think better of yourselves than you should but to see yourselves
first of all as servants of others, whose mission is measured by the
spiritual strength you are given. You are called into membership
in the church which is the living body of Christ and that body
cannot carry out its mission if each one acts alone. A body cannot
function properly if all its members act in the same way; not all can
be leaders and not all can be simple followers, nor do all leaders
have the same role, nor can all followers simply wait to be asked
to serve. Let us use the various gifts we are given cooperatively
with others so that the whole body is effective in bearing witness
to others and serving the needs of the world. If you are a pastor,

care for those committed to your charge; if you are a preacher, proclaim a gospel that changes lives and transforms your society; if you are a lay leader, seek to serve the community around you; if you are a teacher, help others to understand the gospel; if you have gifts of time or money, use those gifts generously to serve human needs; whatever gifts you are given, use them to serve the church and the community so that others will speak well of the church.

Let the unfailing love of God be visible in your life. Be kind to all those you meet and be patient with the angry and hostile; try to understand their point of view and respond gently to those who are angry, for scripture teaches us that "a gentle answer turns away wrath."[20]

Build up daily your relationship with your community; let God's love for you be shared with others; seek ways to serve others and respond to their needs before taking care for yourself; serve eagerly when you are asked and not with reluctance. Contribute not only to the support of your church but to those outside and unknown to you also. When others hurt you, respond with blessing. Find ways to create a stronger and more harmonious community. When others mourn, weep with them; when they celebrate, rejoice with them.

Always leave room for God, who sees far more deeply than we, to have the last word, whether of judgment or praise. Never let yourselves be defeated by the evil around you, but overcome all adversity with love.

13

As the church is a living body, so also a nation is more than a collection of individuals each concerned only for itself. First of all, then, honor those chosen to serve in positions of leadership; they are human beings as you are and they will fail as all sinful human beings fail and as you yourself will often fail, but in honoring them you encourage them to honor and serve you and you contribute to the unity of the nation.

God alone can command our final allegiance but in honoring our leaders we seek to model our human commonwealth on the heavenly realm in which love controls and transforms all relationships. Government exists to serve the members of the community; in condemning it we condemn ourselves and in limiting its ability to act, we limit our ability to provide for the needs of our fellow citizens. Let criticism be constructive and put aside anger and impatience in public discourse. When you pay your taxes, you enable the government to serve the society.

Those who govern are called to preserve order in a sinful world; it is their duty to restrain our worst impulses. It is also true that those who govern are as sinful as any others and must be called to account when they fail, as they will, through self-seeking and a desire to use power and influence for their own advantage.

Honor those who serve well; restrain those who fail. When you do well, you will receive approval from those in authority; when you fall into sin, be afraid of them for they are given authority specifically to punish those who do wrong.

Make no commitment to anyone else except to love them, for those who love their neighbor have fulfilled the law of God. All the commandments and all human law are summed up in the one command to love God and love your neighbor. Love violates no law and creates peace in society.

Remember always that this world with its human structures is passing away and we are called to a new world where we will serve God in peace forever. Let us therefore live now as we hope to live in that coming age. Put aside all self-seeking and indulgence, all quarreling and jealousy, and put on the vestments of worship. Leave behind the works of darkness and walk each day in the light. Let Christ dwell in you and be known to others through your conduct.

14

Welcome all those who come to you seeking a faith to strengthen them but avoid divisive quarrels over opinions. Some whose faith is weak insist on certain kinds of music or take offense over minor matters; they want everything to be as it was in the congregation where they grew up or where they first came to faith. Those whose faith is strong, on the other hand, may see no need to be concerned about these matters. Some want to develop new patterns of worship while others want to continue to do things as they have always been done. God is at work in both weak and strong and it is only God who will judge us. Both must seek first to honor God and make every effort to accommodate the other for God is honored in many ways and no human patterns will satisfy everyone nor will the best we can offer be worthy to compare with the worship we will offer one day in heaven.

Who then is in a position to scorn the offering brought by others? If they seek sincerely to worship God, it is God who will judge and we should never criticize the service of others. Christ who is Lord of all is served in many ways. Every human being, Jew and Gentile, Christian and Muslim, believer and non-believer, will stand before God's judgment seat. Let us therefore be careful never to offend those who belong to God or act in such a way that they feel their best offering has been rejected.

I know that God is honored in many ways and can be worshiped in great simplicity as well as in elaborate ceremonies; God is honored by the music of the past and by the new music of our own day. Those who provide food for the hungry and housing for the homeless are servants of Jesus Christ and so are those who spend their days in prayer, for the gifts of the Spirit are various and all are to be received with thankfulness and used according to the ability each is given. It is not for us to judge those for whom Christ died; they are his servants and he alone is able to judge us all.

Let us then seek for ways to serve God in unity for the world will know us to be servants of Christ only if we are united in love for him and live in peace with each other. Take care that nothing you do offends another Christian or turns them away from the way of faith. Let all that you do be done to express your faith for whatever does not come from faith is sin and separates us from God and from each other.

15

Those of us whose faith is strong must be willing to suffer for the cause of unity because Scripture tells us that the servant of God may be "despised and rejected" by others as, indeed, Christ Jesus was "a man of suffering and acquainted with infirmity"; so then, as he has "borne our infirmities and carried our diseases,"[21] we also must be prepared to bear with the weaker and more difficult members of the community. These Scriptures were written for our guidance and encouragement so that by patient study of that which was written in other times we might increase our faith and be strengthened by a living hope. May the God of hope fill you with all joy and peace in believing through the power of the Holy Spirit so that you may with united hearts and minds and voices give praise to that God revealed to us in Christ Jesus our Lord.

Welcome one another therefore as Christ has welcomed us without regard for our weaknesses and failures for he is able to forgive, renew, and strengthen us so that he may be made known to the whole world through us. For the Psalmist foresees a day when

All the families of the nations shall worship before him[22]
and he also says
   as a father has compassion on his children,
   so does the Lord have compassion on those who fear him,[23]
and Isaiah says,
   the ends of the earth tremble, they draw near and come.[24]
And in another place he says,
   I have given you as a covenant to the peoples,
   a light to the nations.[25]

May the God who created all people and formed them in the image and likeness of God enable us to bear the kind of witness that will break down the divisions among us and enable us to work side by side with those who will at last be joined with us in the perfect worship of the everlasting realm.

I have great confidence in you, dear friends, that you are filled with love and knowledge and able to grow in grace. Nonetheless I have been bold enough to write to you at some length on certain points if only to remind you of these things as God has given me words to explain them. My calling is to serve as a witness to Christ Jesus among all nations and in my priestly ministry to see that their offering is acceptable to God having been sanctified by the Holy Spirit. I rejoice that God has given me strength to bear witness to the gospel in Europe and Asia and now also in America. I will speak only of what Christ has accomplished through my ministry so that in all these regions I have been able to proclaim the whole gospel of God both by word and by deed. It is my hope to continue to make known the good news where it has not yet been heard so that

Those who have never been told of him shall see,
   and those who have never heard of him shall understand.[26]

I will not come to you then as to those who have not known
the gospel but rather to share God's blessing with you so that we
may be mutually strengthened and so that I may be renewed by
your fellowship before I go on to Texas and California. Meanwhile
I must return to Jerusalem to bring gifts from the churches to
the poor among the saints in that place because they make their
witness in the midst of great difficulties. As we have received
spiritual gifts from them it is right that we share with them our
material blessings. Pray earnestly for me that this ministry may
be effective in bringing peace to a troubled region where there are
many who call on God but too few who remember mercy. May the
God of peace who calls us to be peacemakers be with all of you.
Amen.

THE FIRST LETTER TO CALIFORNIA

(I CORINTHIANS)

Dear Friends in California,

Since God has called me to serve him as an ambassador of Jesus Christ, I salute you who are also called to be saints, who call on Jesus as Lord, whether in California or anywhere else—all those who are set apart in Christ Jesus. May grace fill your lives and may you know the peace that comes from God our Father and the Lord Jesus Christ.

I give thanks to God constantly for you because you have been growing in ability to understand and share the gospel of God through the grace that has been given to you in Christ Jesus so that you also can be witnesses to him and lack nothing you need to serve Christ now where you are. God is able to give you the gifts you need in these difficult days as we await the final revelation of our Lord Jesus Christ so that when that last day comes you will be fully prepared. The God who called you into the fellowship of Christ's body the church is faithful and will not leave you in spiritual need.

Since God has given us such gifts, I beg you to live in unity and peace with a common mind and purpose. I have been upset to receive reports of divisions among you and to hear that some call themselves evangelicals and some fundamentalists and some Baptists and Methodists and Roman Catholics and many other names while still others say they are followers of particular pastors or congregations. I am told that some of you will not work together in a common cause and that some will not come together even at the Lord's Table but insist that worship must be ordered in a particular way or that members should subscribe to a specific creed or agree to support certain causes and candidates for public office. These actions dishonor the Lord who died and rose again to save us from the divisions and hostilities of this present world. For if you are as divided among yourselves as the nonbelievers, what evidence do you give the world of our unity in Christ? If we are divided in the eyes of the world, I fear Christ died in vain and my preaching has been in vain.

Do you not yet understand the power of the gospel of Christ crucified? I spent many years studying the wisdom of my ancestors and have studied also the wisdom of this world. The church has produced many wise men and women who have expounded eloquently the gospel message, but to rely on human teaching is to empty the cross of its power. At last the wisdom of God is foolishness to humans and the wisdom of human beings leads only to factions and disputes. If God had meant to save the world by wisdom, there were scholars enough for the purpose, but God has chosen instead to save the world by the foolishness of the gospel.

The way of the world is to seek to save itself by riches and power and knowledge but no wealth that can be piled up secures anyone against the jealousy and greed of others; the rebelliousness of human beings is beyond the power of the strongest nation to control, and the wisdom of the greatest scientists has only produced ever more dangerous weapons. But God's wisdom is wiser than human wisdom, God's power is greater than all human strength, and the riches of God are beyond anything gained from stocks and bonds. We preach the cross of Christ that confounds the world's wisdom and defeats all human power, but is riches and strength for all those who rely on the cross alone.

Consider, my friends, how often the churches have relied on the power and wisdom of human preaching and have measured success by numbers rather than by their impact on the community around them where the poor still remain in poverty and the hungry are not fed; but Jesus our Lord is present in the weak and the poor and not in the congregations of the comfortable. I ask you to notice how the effective witness of the church bears no relationship to the wealth or wisdom of its members but is often most effective where it is poor and persecuted and suffering for lack of earthly power. Remember that Moses also bears witness that God does not choose by numbers or power but only because of love.

<h1 style="text-align:center">2</h1>

Wherever I go, I am determined not to rely on persuasive preaching or human reason but simply to present Christ crucified and to speak of the mystery of the wisdom of God so that you will respond by the power of God's Holy Spirit moving you from within and so that your faith will not rest on any human wisdom, a wisdom that passes away, but on the power of God that endures forever.

Where there are scholars, I will debate with them, but I will not attempt to use the wisdom and logic of this age. That wisdom, like that of past ages, will have its day and be scorned by its own children as out of date. I will speak instead of the mystery of the cross, and it is not my words that will persuade them but God's Spirit moving within. Every one of us is different and no two will be persuaded by the same logic; we ourselves cannot see clearly what it is that we find persuasive though we understand ourselves much better than others do. God's Spirit, however, knows us better than we know ourselves and can work deep within to persuade and transform, to renew and enlighten, to make of us a holy, distinct, and transformed people in whom God is able to carry out the divine purpose.

All this will seem only foolishness to those outside, in whom the Spirit has found no place to work, for the prophet Isaiah says, "My thoughts are not your thoughts nor are your ways my ways."[27]

It is by the Spirit of the Lord and not the human spirit that the mind of the Lord is known—and the Spirit moves most often among the outcast and poor, for Scripture tells us that God's will is done "not by might, nor by power, but by my Spirit."[28]

There is great wealth in your state and the rich have built themselves great mansions but the Spirit of God is not there. There are also large and ornate churches but the Spirit of God is not there either. God lives instead in those who are homeless in order to humble those who have homes and God has chosen to be present among the poor in order to humble those who are rich. God is at work also in other nations and among those outside your borders who seek to enter: would you erect barriers against those in whom God's Holy Spirit chooses to rest? When you who are followers of Christ are divided, how will you be able to overcome the divisions among nations? Do you suppose that God has enriched you for your own sake or to enable you to serve others?

3

I appeal to you, dear friends, to turn your attention to the simplest fundamentals of our faith. Begin again as children since you are acting like children in your pettiness and divisions. Your behavior is guided by the desires of the physical body and not by the leading of the Spirit. Isn't it really your material body you seek to satisfy when you throng the shopping malls and build ever larger houses to live in? When one of you says, "I belong to Luther" and another says, "I belong to Calvin" and another says, "I belong to John Wesley" or the Pope or Rick Warren or Robert Schuller, are you not merely human? Who are Rick or Robert or Paul except servants through whom you came to believe as God led you by the Spirit. So then neither one nor another of these is anything but only God who is at work in you through the Spirit. It may be that one plants the seed and another waters it while still another brings in the harvest, but all of these are laborers working toward a common purpose and serving the same God.

We could also say that one has laid the foundation and another has set up the walls while still another has furnished the building, but all of these, again, are simply laborers. There is no other foundation than Jesus Christ and whatever is built on that foundation will be tested to prove its worth. If walls of division are built or a roof for your own protection, such building will not last for it is not the work of the Spirit who sends us out and offers us no protection against the world except the strength to love. The cathedral that is built today to glorify its founder will be bankrupt and sold to others tomorrow but the man or woman who seeks to serve the Lord Christ builds a temple that will last for ever.

Do you not know that you yourselves are God's temple and that your bodies are made holy by God's Spirit in you? But how will others see who you are if you set out to shape yourselves after the fashion of this world? When you rely on worldly accomplishment and distinction, what will the world see except a reflection of itself? It is instead in foolishness and weakness that God is made known through us; it is when we put off our worldly clothing and adornment that the Spirit is able to shine through.

Do not be deceived, my friends: whoever it is that ministers to you is your servant. Whether it is Peter or Paul or someone else, they belong to you and you belong to Christ and Christ belongs to God.

4

You might think of us then as servants of Christ who have been entrusted with a gift as managers of a fund, and it is required of such managers that they be faithful in their trust. They must answer only to the source of the fund. So it is irrelevant to me what human critics may say and I do not judge myself. The day will come when I must answer to the Lord who has given me gifts to use in serving and when that day comes whatever we have done will be brought to light.

I apply this to myself and to others who serve you in ministry so that you can apply the same standard to yourselves. What do you have that you were not given, whether it is the various talents you have or the gift of life itself? So how can you boast of anything, whether in your employment or your possessions or your friends? It may be inevitable that Americans in general and, perhaps, Californians in particular feel uniquely blessed; the fact remains that you have nothing you were not given to hold and use as stewards or managers, and the day will come when you will be called to account for the use you have made of it.

Do you really think that you rule the world? I wish you did so I could share it with you. You rejoice in your strength while we give thanks for our weakness; you exult in your wisdom while we can only point to our foolishness; you are honored while we are scorned. I sometimes think that God has set us up to be mocked by the world of wealth and fashion. Even now we are hungry and thirsty and homeless. Nevertheless when we are cursed, we bless, and when we are slandered by others we speak kindly of them; when we are rejected and treated as the very dregs of humanity, we endure it all for your sake, for although you have many pastors and teachers, I alone have been sent to you as an apostle of Jesus Christ. I am not saying all this to embarrass you but to get your attention and for your benefit.

I appeal to you then to imitate me and those faithful pastors I send you who come not to lord it over you but to serve you and to remind you of the gospel I teach in all the churches. I know that many are faithful, but some are arrogant and doubt I will ever come; but I am coming soon, God willing, and I will see whether those who set themselves up as someone important have deeds that match their arrogant words. For the rule of God is not to be seen in arrogant boasting and pride but in humble acts of service and the Spirit's power. What would you prefer: shall I come to you in anger and judgment or in love and thankful praise?

5

I am deeply grieved to hear that some of you are unfaithful in your sexual relationships, forming brief relationships and then divorcing and marrying again or, sometimes, not marrying at all. Yes, and some who act in this way condemn others whose relationships are faithful but untraditional. How is it possible that you accept those who act unfaithfully and condemn those who are faithful? There are nonbelievers who do better than that! I may not be present with you at the moment, but I know what is happening and have given my judgment as if I were there. You cannot continue to include in your number those who fail to make a faithful commitment and yet despise others who do. Have you not understood how quickly disease spreads through a body? It's like yeast in a lump of dough as it transforms the whole, so purge out the corrupting leaven so that the body is renewed and pure. The Passover custom is to throw the old leaven away and begin the new year with new bread. In the same way, Christ died to sin and rose again in a clean and renewed body free from the stain of evil. Let the church, Christ's body, also be cleansed of sin and renewed in holiness so that we may celebrate the resurrection feast with none of the leaven of arrogance and unfaithfulness but with the new, unleavened bread of truth and faithfulness.

I wrote to you once before to say that you should avoid contact, so far as possible, with people whose lives are undisciplined or self-seeking, who indulge in drugs or sexual promiscuity or exploit the poor. I meant, of course, the unbelievers around you whom you cannot avoid completely. I write to you now to tell you to have nothing at all to do with those who call themselves Christians but are, in fact, no better than the unbelievers, whose daily lives show no evidence of the Spirit's transforming power, who are self-centered, not Christ-centered, who love money more than their neighbor. It is for God, not for us, to judge the nonbeliever, but we must be discerning within the church and hold up such a standard of faithfulness that Christ will be seen in our common life.

6

It is shameful that Christians become so badly divided that they cannot resolve a matter without going to the public courts. To have such disputes at all is a defeat. We are to be known as people of peace, working together in common cause, bound together in love. Why then can you not resolve whatever differences arise? Why not let yourselves be wronged? To go to human courts at all is evidence of your failure to live together in peace. When such a failure involves disputes over church property surely it should be possible to find impartial judges among yourselves and agree to accept their decision. Are there none among you who are wise enough to judge such matters in a way acceptable to all?

I should not need to remind you that all wrongdoers will be judged at last in a higher court. Those who defraud and deceive others, who traffic in sex, who abuse the vulnerable, who exploit those who work for them, who see their neighbor's need but give no assistance—as some of you have done in time past—will stand before the Lord Jesus on the final day and have no excuse for what they have done. But you have been washed in the waters of baptism and sanctified by the Holy Spirit and redeemed by the cross of Christ. Live, then, like those whom Christ has justified.

You say that we are set free by the knowledge of a loving Lord who will understand our failures and forgive us. That may be true, but it is no excuse for those who knowingly offend. We are not subject to dietary laws; we are free to eat whatever we want, yes, but not all food is beneficial; we need to be wise in our choices. Those who suffer poverty may still be poor no matter how much we give but that is no excuse for indulging ourselves and failing to do what we can to help them. Likewise the desires of the body are often indulged without thought of either earthly or eternal consequences but God made the body to serve and will raise it up at the last day. Don't you know that your bodies are members of Christ? Can I then take the members of Christ and use them simply to satisfy my desires? Those desires were created to enable us to express our love through our human flesh, to give myself to another not first for my own pleasure. Self-control deepens our human affections while self-indulgence is finally destructive of the body. Other sins we commit are outside the body but sexual indulgence is a sin against the body. Don't you know that your body is the temple of the indwelling Holy Spirit that is God's gift to you? You do not belong to yourself; you were bought with a price; so let your body be used to praise God.

7

Now let me deal with the questions you asked in your letter to me. Marriage and sexual relationships are not essential to human life; sexual desires are subject to our control though individuals may differ in the strength of those desires. I have not married and have, as a result, been free to carry out my ministry more fully. Some of you also may be called to celibacy and should be grateful; it is a gift of freedom, a freedom in which we can be fully obedient to the Lord we serve.

Not all, however, have that gift and those not called to celibacy should marry. Marriage also is a gift of freedom for the passions can be centered on one and married persons can learn by giving themselves fully to each other the joy to be found in faithful relationship, for the relationship of marriage is an image of the relationship between Christ and the church. Love is most fully expressed in faithfulness; those who are unfaithful do not know love. They are controlled by their passions, enslaved by their desires; but the married rejoice in the freedom of selfless obedience to another.

Christian marriage is devotion to one, for Christ is one; the followers of Christ who are joined in marriage become one body; they express in a material way their spiritual unity and are strengthened in that unity by their unity in the body of Christ.

In former times, this was not the case; we read of our ancestors, Abraham, Isaac, Jacob, David, and Solomon who were united with wives and servants and concubines for, whatever some may say, the Scriptures do not teach marriage between one man and one woman. In Islam also, marriage may include more than one partner since Muslims do not teach the unity of the body of Christ, but in Christ two are made one and learn faithfulness to one.

As to faithful marriage between two men or between two women, I find no guidance in Scripture. Promiscuity and all self-indulgence are, of course, condemned; God is faithful and those made in God's image are to embody God's faithfulness. No marriage is, in itself, a holy thing any more than any other human relationship. If, however, two people who are one in Christ desire to commit themselves and their relationship to God in marriage, why should the church not ask God's blessing on that relationship? We are children of grace, not of law, and where grace is present, it is our role to give thanks and bless.

A divorce is always evidence of failure and should be mourned, not celebrated. The marriage blessing should be given only to those who are known to the church as stable and faithful people, whose deeper relationship will strengthen the church and be evidence to the world of the power of God's Spirit to transform human lives. Partners who are unfaithful or who indulge themselves in drugs or who are abusive are to be admonished and counseled with prayer. If their lives are changed, the church is strengthened but if they continue in their former ways, the partner should be free to divorce; it is as if the relationship were between a believer and an unbeliever: the believer should not be bound to the one who resists the Spirit. It is to peace that God has called you. The believing partner may save the unbeliever if it is God's will but he or she must be concerned for themselves and their children and the peace of the community. This is the rule I give to all the churches. It is my own rule, not the Lord's, but I believe I am following the Spirit's guidance.

New converts should be encouraged to remain where they are for the time being and to make no drastic changes immediately unless they were living a life of sin. Some are eager to become pastors and teachers at once or to take leadership positions in the congregation; some even are eager to abandon their work and find new occupations that they believe are more appropriate for Christians. I would encourage new Christians to continue in whatever position they now have for the time being. We do not know how much time remains but we know we are called to be faithful now and to serve God where we are. There is more need of faithful bankers and lawyers than of ushers and more ministry to be performed by cheerful clerks, mechanics, and secretaries than by members of a church committee. Our ministry is first of all in and to the world; it is the role of the congregation to discern ministries and call out those whose gifts they recognize.

If you are engaged to be married or if you hope to begin a family and you are convinced that God is calling you to undertake these responsibilities, then you should carry out the plans you have made. But don't do it if you are uncertain. It is good for many to marry and it is good for many not to marry. Those who marry can come to a deeper understanding of love and can raise up children to serve God. Those who do not marry are freed from the many anxieties of family life and can give themselves more fully to God's service. Married or unmarried, you can serve God now where you are. I would spare you the anxieties of additional commitments, especially those that would reduce your ability to serve God in the church.

Never rush into new roles or relationships but serve patiently where you are. Never take on responsibilities that would detract from your family life or your ministry within the church. The man or woman who attains high office but has no time for their family or their church is seeking glory for themselves and not for God.

8

Now as to food and drink that some reject because they feel wiser than others, it is useful to remember that "knowledge puffs up but love builds up." There are many today who believe that we should never eat the flesh of animals. They have studied the matter and may well be able to teach others a better way, yet some exalt themselves and despise others and so divide the church to the great harm of those whom they reject. A diet is useful but no diet takes God's place in our lives. There is only one God, from whom all life comes and for whom all life exists; some however exalt their beliefs into God's place and worship their beliefs rather than God. I think it is wrong to offend others over such matters; we need to be more considerate of those with whom we differ and recognize the danger of destroying their faith when they find some adopting a superior attitude. Hold your beliefs, indeed, but be careful not to offend.

In the same way, it is important to be considerate of those who cannot safely use alcohol. It may be that you can drink safely, but it is vital to remember those who cannot. When you give a party, be sure that there are nonalcoholic beverages easily and equally available so that no one is made to feel of less importance than others. God has created a variety of food and drink both for enjoyment and nourishment and I can in good conscience enjoy them all, but certain foods and drink may be harmful to some and all of them are harmful if not used in moderation. Be careful, then, to provide wisely for your own body and for the church, the body of Christ. I will never eat or drink anything that might cause my brother or sister to fall.

9

If you recognize me as an apostle, I trust I may say something about the ministry to which I am called and in which I serve. Surely I have as much right as any other Christian to be married and to earn my living, but if I am commissioned to preach the gospel, do I not also have the right to be free of material possessions? A soldier in military service surely has the right to be paid, but one who serves the country is not free to exploit that position for personal gain. If I choose to support myself, I do it to be free to serve yet I would not want others to feel they must do the same nor would I want you to feel that you have no need to support those who minister to you. It is right to make proper provision for the ministers of the gospel but it is unseemly for anyone to grow rich in material things from the ministry they are given. You must see that those who serve you are free to do so and not burdened with financial cares. Surely anyone who builds up a small business expects to earn an income from their work and the one who invests money carefully is entitled to some return. In just the same way, a farmer expects to benefit from the crop he produces and the one who plants an orchard expects to eat some of the fruit. So also those who plant the gospel seed and nurture the young crop are entitled to some benefit from their work. Those who are called to ministries in the church should be able to serve in that ministry without undue concern for their material needs. Those who serve, however, must not allow themselves to be enslaved by a desire for wealth or fail to set an example of charitable, indeed sacrificial, giving. If Jesus gave his life for us, we must surely be willing to endure some privation in his service.

Although I have a right to compensation for my service, I have made no use of those rights. I want to be free of obligations to anyone except the Lord I serve. I am free of obligations to any so that I may become the servant of all. I seek especially to serve those who have no one to serve them. For the sake of the homeless I have become homeless myself and for the sake of the immigrant I have become one without rights of citizenship. For the sake of the unemployed, I have put aside my usual employment and joined bread lines and turned to soup kitchens. Where any are despised, I have stood with them. To those without hope, I have brought a word of hope and to those who feel secure in their own achievements I have brought the witness of a life dependent entirely on God. I have made myself the servant of all so that by all means I might bring them the gospel.

In any marathon, there are many who enter but only one who wins, yet all those who compete submit themselves to discipline so that their running has a purpose. They do it to gain a sense of physical achievement but I do it to gain an eternal reward. If you train yourself and submit to discipline for the transitory accomplishment, how much more should we train and discipline ourselves to attain eternal life? I do not run aimlessly but I live a disciplined and committed life so that the life I proclaim to others may be mine for ever.

10

I want you to understand very clearly, my friends, that no earthly rite or experience can guarantee your salvation. Surely you know the Scriptural story of how God brought the people of Israel out of slavery in Egypt only to find later that they were enslaving others. The prophets proclaimed to them God's priority of justice and warned them not to oppress the poor but they continued to heap up riches for themselves and to pay no attention to the needs of those around them. Therefore God sent the armies of other nations to defeat them and carry them into exile for those whom God has chosen and enlightened have a greater responsibility to serve human need. The poor, the unemployed, the hungry, the homeless, the stranger and immigrant in your midst, all these also are children of God. They may differ in color or language or religion, but they are all the children of God and should be a first concern for those of you who are comfortable and secure. If it is by your wisdom and skill that you have provided so well for yourself, who gave you that wisdom and skill? Do you not see that God's gifts are not given as a reward but as a trust? At the judgment you will not be asked how well you have cared for yourself but what you have done for others. Those whom God calls, who are washed in baptism and nourished with God's word and fed at God's table have the greatest responsibility. God loves you and cares for you and expects you to love and care for others. So if you think you are doing well, be careful; you may need to repent, and judgment is always at hand, but God will not allow you to be tested beyond your ability.

Remember also that the bread we break is a sharing in the body of Christ and that we who are Christians, many as we are and diverse in our ways of worship and praise, are nevertheless one body because we share the communion bread. If we are thus united in Christ, nothing else has a prior claim on our time, our allegiance, or our resources. We are Christians first and Americans second; we are Christians first and union members second; we are Christians first and sports fans second. The people of Israel were condemned for sharing in sacrifices to idols; how shall we escape judgment if we make sacrificial offerings of our time and money to the false gods of our culture? You cannot drink the cup of the Lord and the cup of demons. You cannot partake of the table of the Lord and the table of demons. You cannot pay more for sports events than you give to your church or spend more at restaurants than you give to the poor. Nothing is evil in itself, but not all things are beneficial. You may say that "All things are lawful," but not everything is constructive. Never seek only your own advantage but seek first how to serve others.

Remember always that you are a witness to the gospel of Christ and that others will be influenced by your example. You are free to take part in the feasts and celebrations of others, but if you should learn that the food or drink you are offered has been produced by exploiting others, it may be better to abstain. You have done nothing wrong yourself but you may seem to approve of the wrong doing of others and so imply that your faith makes no difference and that others likewise can be indifferent to injustice. So, whether you eat or drink, or whatever you do, do everything for the glory of God.

Give no offense to believers or to nonbelievers or to the church of God. In everything I do, I try to seek no advantage for myself, but always that of others, so that they may be brought to believe.

11

Try to follow my example, as I try to follow the example of Christ. I commend you for reading my letters to all the churches and seeking to follow my guidance but you need to understand that the guidance I have given others may not be applicable to you. If I wrote to other Christians that a woman should wear a hat in church and that a man should not pray with his head covered, it was because that was customary among worshipers there and it seemed to create a needless obstacle for Christians to abandon familiar customs in matters of little importance. Even in writing to such churches, however, I have also pointed out that among Christians male and female are essentially equal. It may be that the first woman was made from the first man but ever since that time men have come from women. But God is the source of all and all are alike in God's sight. In your culture, it would create an unnecessary barrier to faith if women were required to cover their heads or not encouraged to play a full part in the ordained ministry so, in your community, you should be careful to provide equal roles for all.

You are free to dress as you please, but again, so as to cause no offense, it is best to dress as others do. If some wish to argue about such matters, look for common ground; you can say on my authority that there is no such custom in any of the congregations of God's people.

One thing I will not praise you for is this: that when you come together for the Lord's Supper, it is not for the better but for the worse. At the very time when you should be most united, you are instead most divided for you say, "Unless you believe exactly what I believe," or "Unless you recognize the same chief pastors I do, we cannot share this meal." There will always be differences among you; it is only in debating differences that we grow in understanding;

but if you cannot share this meal it is not the Lord's Supper that you receive.

Are you not all followers of Christ? Are you not all baptized? Do you not desire to be fed at the Lord's table? Why then do you place fences around your tables to keep out your fellow Christians? Shall I then commend you for your concern with divisive issues? I cannot commend you at all.

Surely you ought to discuss the meaning of this meal and the nature of leadership in the church but how will we be more united if we are not all sharers in the same meal? You live in a new age that uses language in new ways yet you are divided by the language of the past and formulas that few today even understand. I appeal to you to move on and bear witness in your angry and divided world to the power of the Spirit to create unity among us.

I passed on to you what I received from the Lord, that on the night in which he was betrayed he took a loaf of bread, gave thanks for it, broke it, and gave it to his friends saying, "This is my body; it is given for you; do this in recognition of my unifying presence." After supper he did much the same thing with the cup saying, "This cup renews God's ancient covenant with God's people by means of my blood. Whenever you drink it, recognize my unifying presence." That is why, whenever you eat this bread and drink from this cup, you proclaim Christ's death and recognize his presence in your midst.

How, then, can you be divided when you do this? Can you bear witness to unity when you are so obviously divided? If the world is to be judged for its age-old enmities and divisions, how much more the church? Would it not be better to judge ourselves and reform ourselves than to be judged by the Lord? Think carefully about what you are doing and come together with clear consciences having sacrificed your narrow concerns for the common good. I will have more to say about this when I come.

12

I need to tell you some things about the work of the Holy Spirit. You should be aware first of all, that not everyone who invokes the name of Jesus does so by the power of the Spirit. There are some who call on that name for their own purposes, whether it be financial gain or worldly fame. Avoid people like that; they bring dishonor on the gospel and will be called to account in the end. Jesus did not live in luxury, nor do I or the other apostles. A simple style of life serves the gospel best.

There are various gifts that the Spirit pours out on us, but all for the unity and well-being of the church. Some are given gifts for leadership, others for serving the needs of the poor, others for administration, still others for teaching or preaching or healing or mission. Some are given technical skills and others are given musical ability, some are enabled to speak in tongues, but all these are gifts of the same Spirit who gives these gifts for the building up of the church, the body of Christ.

You know how the various members of the human body work together for the well being of the whole; so it is with the church. Whatever our background or education or race or national origin, we are baptized into one body and know each other as fellow servants of Christ. Whatever church or congregation we belong to, still we are members of one body and the Roman Catholic cannot say to the Baptist, or the Methodist to the Episcopalian, "I have no need of you," nor can the wealthy executive say to the homeless person or illegal immigrant, "I have no need of you." The body is composed of many members but all must work together for the body's health. Just as in a race, the runner needs not only strong legs but a healthy heart and disciplined mind, so the members of the body must work together for the common good and none can prosper when some are in need. If there is cancer in one organ, the whole body suffers; if one member is honored all can rejoice. So too in the church, if a pastor is self-seeking or a congregation shows no concern for the needy, all pastors and Christian people will find their own witness less effective and their neighbors less open to the gospel. Not all those who speak in Jesus's name do so by the power of the Spirit but all who do so make a difference to the health of the body.

Now you are the body of Christ and each of you is a member of that body and each of you is called to a ministry. A few are called to positions of leadership as pastors and teachers, some are called to serve as missionaries and evangelists, some as choir members and ushers and such roles within the congregation, but all are called to serve the needs of the world and bear witness to the gospel where Christ is not known or the gospel is scorned. The gifts of the Spirit are many and each member is given gifts to serve in particular ways. Not all are to be pastors, not all are to be teachers, not all have gifts of healing or evangelism, but work to use the gift you are given for the good of the whole church.

Above all things, remember that you are called to serve, not to rule. Do not listen to those who hope to control your society by enacting laws governing sexual conduct or proclaiming Christ in secular schools or invoking Christ in political debates. Faith is made known by love not laws or outward display. Let me remind you of the words of a familiar hymn that speaks of a better way:

13

If I should speak with angels' tongues
and the archangel's voice,
But still I have no love, then all
I do is make a noise;
And if I have prophetic powers

and faith and knowledge so
That mountains move, but have no love
I still have need to grow.
True love is patient, love is kind,
not envious or rude.
Love is not selfish, does not boast,
and loves to hear the truth.
Love bears all things, believes all things,
endures what foes may send;
There is no limit to its hope,
and love will never end.
Both prophecies and tongues will cease,
and knowledge has its day,
But when the perfect morning breaks
all else will pass away.
For now we see as if through glass,
but then, by God's good grace,
We will, with all God's chosen ones
see Jesus face to face.
Three things there are of which God's own
must always be possessed:
These things are hope and faith and love,
but love is always best.

14

Make love the center of your life and work to develop spiritual gifts, especially those of worship and prayer. Love is centered on others, especially your fellow Christians, but too often I hear that your worship is centered on yourself and seeks emotional rewards rather than spiritual growth. You have been more concerned with growth in numbers than with growth in the deep things of the spirit.

You measure a congregation by attendance and provide convenient parking, comfortable seating, and the music of the secular world yet your divorce rate is growing, poverty is increasing, and anger and divisiveness are more evident every year. I see little difference between the lives Christians live and the lives of those around you. Those who worship in this way satisfy themselves but true worship challenges us to change and does indeed change us through the power of the Spirit.

Dear friends, if I come to you with exciting music, how will I benefit you unless I bring you some teaching of Scripture or insight into a life of prayer? When you go to a concert, you get involved in the music and are aroused to a sense of happiness that may continue for some time afterwards, but does it change who you are? So, too, if I go to church to worship and the music arouses a sense of joy, that is all very well, but do I know God better as a result? Is it Jesus who fills me with joy or is it only the beat of the music? I would like all of you to be filled with joy, but even more I would like you to be filled with the Spirit.

I must also ask you to consider whether you truly take part in the worship that is offered or whether you have become spectators who come only to be entertained. It is all too easy for the leaders of worship to become performers, whether a priest at the altar or a preacher in the pulpit, a musician at the organ or a rock band on the stage. It is well for them to offer their gifts to God and for the congregation to offer it with them, but it is very easy to sit back and let them perform for us rather than for God. When this happens, the church ceases to be a body in which the several members work together for the benefit of all and offer themselves to God, but instead the church becomes controlled by one member or ministry while the other members exist for the benefit of the one.

My sisters and brothers, we must become adults in our worship and no longer children excited by every passing fancy. Be childlike in trust and in joyfulness, but in thinking and spiritual growth you must become adults whose wisdom and faithfulness need no artificial stimulation but are strong enough to withstand the trends that are popular and return to the rock on which you were built at first. Use new music as well as old but be sure that the words speak wisdom to the mind as well so that you will continue to sing God's goodness during the week. Let your worship be clear and simple so that all can take part easily and understand what is done. Proclaim the word with the power of God's Spirit and come to the Lord's Table to be renewed in strength and unity.

Let no one be excluded from your worship on the basis of gender or race or national origin. Does not Moses command that the festival be celebrated not only by your sons and daughters but also by the stranger in your midst?[29] Since it is the custom in your society for leadership to be shared equally by men and women, let it be the same in the community of the saints for God does not make distinctions among persons.

If you have great buildings for worship, you should rejoice to use them but you must remember that God is worshiped as well in the simplest home, or hospital room, or in nursing homes and prisons. Wherever you are, whatever the circumstances, offer the best that you have remembering that the Lord Jesus was well content to share the meals of the rich and poor, the honored and the outcast alike. Let all your acts of worship, at all times and in all places, be offered with dignity and joy.

15

I want you to understand, dear friends, the confidence we have for those who have died so that your sorrow will not be like the sorrow of those who have no hope. The ancient Creed that many of you recite—that Jesus "on the third day rose again from the

dead"—is a summary of the Creed I recorded in one of my early
letters: "that he was buried, and that he was raised on the third day
in accordance with the scriptures, and that he appeared to Cephas,
then to the twelve, then to more than five hundred brothers and
sisters at one time." This statement remains central to our faith, for
if Jesus has not been raised, my preaching is in vain and your faith
is pointless. Indeed, we have been proclaiming a falsehood and
deceiving our hearers by proclaiming a resurrection that did not
take place if, indeed, Jesus has not been raised.

That same ancient Creed still states that you believe in "the
resurrection of the body," yet I have heard that some of you do not
affirm the resurrection of the body but, like the ancient Greeks,
affirm instead an immortal soul. If the soul is immortal, however,
what good news is there in the gospel? If the soul is immortal,
why should we fear death? If the soul is immortal, why did God
raise the body of Christ from death? If the soul is immortal, why
do we baptize the bodies of children and new believers and why
do we feed the body at the Lord's Table? Indeed, if the body is
not raised, why are you so careful to care for your bodies and to
concern yourselves with the bodies of those who are hungry and
diseased and dying?

Is it not because God sent the Son into this world in human
flesh that we are able to proclaim the care of God for creation, that
the material world is not an evil to be transcended, mere matter
to be used and misused at our pleasure, but a good creation to be
valued and cared for and redeemed? Consider the lilies, as Jesus
said, and consider all the splendor and wonder of this material
world and the beauty created by flesh and blood: does all this have
no value in the eyes of a Creator who, in the end, values only the
Spirit? No, God has shown us in Christ Jesus that flesh and blood
can be used to redeem the physical body and the material world.
In his body he walked among us, in his body he died for us and

was buried, in his body he rose again and appeared to many still bearing in his body the wounds of the cross.

Through all the ages since, Christians have held fast to their faith in the resurrection of the body. Though their bodies were tortured and burned, yet they believed that God cared for the body and would raise it up at the last. Now, when the body is better nourished and cared for than ever before, why would you believe that it is a worthless shell to be discarded at last while an unseen and unseeable soul lives on?

But some will ask, "What is this resurrection body? How is it to be fed and clothed and in what resurrection world will we live?" These are foolish questions! Cannot the God who created the infinite glory of the universe create also a new world for the risen body? The life we live now is evidence of the manifold ways in which life is changed not ended. Each cell of the physical body is replaced many times in the course of a life. The body we inhabited as children is not the body of the adult nor is the body of the caterpillar the same as that of the butterfly. Life takes many forms and is often transformed in the course of life. The young man gives thanks for a body that can climb mountains and run in a marathon; the older woman gives thanks for a body that can embrace a grandchild and be warmed by the fire; one gives thanks for a voice to sing while another gives thanks for ears to listen and still another gives thanks for hands with which to paint and to carve and to write. Although I can train my body to do many things, there are always many things that others can do with their bodies that I cannot do with mine; a transformed body is not the same body but one that will open to us new gifts beyond what we can now imagine. The prophet Isaiah foresaw God's people gathered at a wedding feast in a transformed world and the prophet John saw the saints crowned in glory and singing praise to God in the resurrection body; but these visions are limited by the life we know

now. No mind can imagine a world we have not known nor can I tell you what the body will be when it is raised in power. What it is, we do not need to ask; we can rest content in this: that it is the habitation prepared for the holy people of God.

Consider the transformations that take place daily and unobserved such as the exchange of matter and energy that your scientists teach: what if the material body becomes pure energy? Is it not still the same body just as your present body is the same body you had when you were young? Remember also that the first human being was formed in God's image and not subject to the power of sin and death. We are no longer what we once were but God in Christ has acted to set us free from those things that constrain us. Adam and all our ancestors in the flesh have bequeathed us a society in which anger and jealousy, envy and hatred, constantly corrupt the good that is in us, yet even now, in the body of Christ, we begin to see the potential of human life. Prophets, martyrs, pastors, evangelists and all the holy people of God, where society is corrupt and where human lives are weighed down by poverty and hatred, bear witness to the power of love to redeem the evil and renew the world. We are in Christ a transformed and transforming body and the Spirit is at work in us now to show us the first evidence of God's purpose. You can see, then, that I am showing you a mystery: we all must die but also we shall all be changed, for this perishable body must be made imperishable and this mortal body must be made immortal. When this earthly body has put on the heavenly body death will be swallowed up in victory. What power does death have if Christ indeed is risen? And what do we have to fear if we are members of his body and are raised with him to new life? Thanks be to God who gives us such a victory through our Lord Jesus Christ! Be faithful, then, and persevere in the faith knowing that your life and labor have an eternal value in the Lord.

16

I am eager to come to you and spend time with you so that we may grow together in faith, but I am unable to come for the present. There is, apparently, a visa problem of some sort, perhaps because of my Middle Eastern origins. The fact of my Roman citizenship has no value in such a world as this so I will be patient and exercise my ministry where I am for the time being. When I come at last I hope to spend some time and not simply pass through. So I will work in Rome until Pentecost since there are many opportunities here and, as usual, much opposition. If Timothy is able to come to you, I trust you will welcome him; he may be young, but he has been an effective witness to the faith so give him your support and send him on his way in peace.

Remember the church in Jerusalem where Christians continue to face great difficulties. Take a special offering every week and be generous. I would rather not need to ask for money when I come. Then, when I arrive, I will send letters to go with your offering and any messengers you choose.

I wanted to send Apollos to you but he is unwilling to go so far at the moment. He will come later when his present work is better established. He is an effective advocate and will be able to strengthen you in your ministry.

Let everything you do be done in love; there is no other way to overcome your divisions and bear witness to the Lord Jesus. Be patient with each other and do your best to overcome whatever keeps you apart. We cannot bear effective witness while there are divisions among us.

I am grateful that you were able to send some of your members to me; they have been of great assistance in many ways and help me feel closer to you in spite of the distance between us. I wish they could stay with me but I know they have their own work to do. They will tell you more about our circumstances when they return to you. The churches here send you their greetings. All the faithful send you greetings and hold you in their prayers. Pray also for them and for all those who hold fast to the faith in times of hardship.

I am writing these words of greeting with my own hand: may those who do not love the Lord be changed. Lord, come! The grace of the Lord Jesus be with you. I send my love to all of you. Amen.

THE SECOND LETTER TO CALIFORNIA

(II CORINTHIANS)

Dear Friends in California,

Timothy and I send greetings in Christ to you and all the faithful Christians throughout your distant part of the world. May grace be yours and peace from God, life-giver and nurturer, and the Lord Jesus Christ in whom alone we live. I give thanks to God who has strengthened us in all the suffering we have experienced in recent weeks so that we are enabled to strengthen you in your sufferings as well. These recent disasters remind us how dependent we are on God for life itself and how in our sufferings we are compelled to learn again how great a gift life is and how little we truly need of the material things around us. It is, we must remember, the crucified Christ who poured out his life for us and continues to summon us into a fellowship of suffering through which the abundance of consolation is made known. If we suffer now for a time, it is for your consolation that we do so and if we are consoled, it is by knowing that you share our sufferings.

The new wave of natural disasters that has swept through your country must teach you the use and meaning of suffering. Some will preach a painless Christ who offers good feelings to those who are comfortable but we preach Christ crucified, the Lord who enables us to face the reality of life; we are not surprised when we are asked to suffer since it is through suffering that we have been offered the salvation that endures. We do not lose hope for you even in the midst of suffering and desolation since it is through suffering that the power of Christ is made known. Those who have nothing left to lose can see most clearly that God's grace is present with them.

We want you to know, dear friends, the depth of suffering we ourselves have passed through in Asia where anger and hostility surrounded us until we were utterly crushed and even despaired of life. Yet in that time of suffering we knew again the renewal of strength that comes from reliance on Christ alone. In the agony of what seemed to be certain death we were able still to turn to Christ who raises the dead; as he rescued us in so hopeless a situation, we know he will rescue us again and that he will also rescue you. Hope and prayer remain the very center of life for us as we are supported by the prayers of so many and join with them in prayer for you. Though human foes assail us in the turmoil of Asia and the forces of nature assail you on the western edge of the world, we remain confident that neither we nor you will be swept away; indeed, we will emerge with new strength having tested God's promises again and learned how unshakable and secure is the life of those who trust in him.

It is against this background that we write to tell you our plans and assure you that we will come to you soon. We have written this before and we write it now again so that you will not imagine that we have changed our intentions. Some may think that we have wavered and that our Yes and No cannot be trusted; let me assure you that we are unwavering in our purpose. We will indeed come to you soon, but we have delayed our visit to allow you time to come together again in common purpose. We do not wish to come to you in judgment and be forced to deal harshly with those we love. When we hear of divisions among you and of some who seek to promote themselves without thought for the body of Christ, we would rather wait until you resolve such matters in our absence. Our love for you is such that we have chosen to wait for a while and let you find a way to call back those who have gone astray or, if necessary, to tell the world that they are not of the truth so that all can see our unity and hear one gospel message. My own purpose is unchanging: I will come, but I hope still to come in thankfulness and peace.

2

Believe me, I have no desire to come again in judgment and cause you pain. Even to write such things to you is painful to me. Who else is there to cause me joy except yourselves and what joy can I find in you when you remain divided? What will I be able to boast of in the last day except yourselves? But what joy can I take in a divided church? Does not division among us make a lie of the very gift of life that we are given in Christ? What can it mean to be baptized into division or to come to the Lord's Supper at separate tables? How can you proclaim a gospel of reconciliation when you remain unreconciled among yourselves? I beg you to consider whether those things that have divided you have more power than the grace in which we stand. Satan indeed is strong and wise in the ways of the world, but we are not ruled by this world's wisdom nor can we be defeated by worldly power or all the forces of spiritual wickedness if we return to the simplicity of the gospel and the foolishness of the faith that is sufficient for all our needs.

How then can you work for reconciliation? Forgiveness is the way to peace. It is easy to condemn and difficult to forgive, but condemnation is for the teachings that divide; forgiveness is for those individuals who have created division.

When we seek reconciliation, it is only in Christ that such an outcome is possible. It is not a choice between the teaching of others and our teaching but rather in the teaching of Christ that we must come together. We come from different understandings and journey by various roads, and Satan would have us look at where we are rather than where we are going. I am well aware of his wiles and you must be also. Our present understanding is limited and can divide us but we must look ahead to the full knowledge of Christ and find our unity there. Love those who

trouble you; if you forgive them, I forgive them also. I forgive
them for your sake and for the sake of the gospel.

In my recent travels I became anxious to know what had become
of Timothy and I changed my travel plans in hope of finding him.
Although Timothy had gone on, I found new openings where I
was and so remained there to build on the opportunities provided:
it is as if the Spirit leads me in a triumphal procession from one
place to the next and the fragrance of the gospel is dispelled
everywhere. Who can explain how this happens or be worthy of
the work God does through us? We never put the gospel up for
sale as some do but speak as those sent from God and standing in
Christ's presence. The fragrance of life draws those God is calling;
let that same fragrance radiate out from your lives also.

3

Can we talk together now on this basis? I hope by now you don't
need letters of reference for me! It seems to me that you yourselves
are whatever letter of reference we need: a living letter of flesh and
blood, better than any form letter sent by fax. God's Spirit has
written a letter in your lives that is better than anything I could
write myself and your lives are visible to be read by anyone.

Do you remember how Moses had to cover his face when he
came down from Mount Sinai with the first commandments
carved on a stone tablet? If letters carved in stone had such glory,
how much more glorious is a letter written in human flesh? When
Mother Teresa labored in the slums of Calcutta, the light from her
ministry was visible throughout the world. When Martin Luther
King, Jr., wrote his letter from a Birmingham jail, it lit up the
American skies and showed many people for the first time the
injustice against which he fought. That is the kind of letter you

need to write to your world. Let people see in your lives the letter God is sending to the world around you.

But you need to understand that there are always those who cannot see the letter because they have blinders on. They are comfortable with the darkened life with which they are familiar and would be dazzled to come out into the bright sun of a new life. They cannot see the world as we see it in the light of Christ. They still look at the world in terms of familiar customs and have no understanding of the freedom given by the Spirit. You see such people every day, looking at their iPads as they go to their jobs, returning home to the dim light of their television screens, and not knowing that there is so much more light available, light that can transform their lives and the world around them.

You struggle to maintain order in your troubled cities and find ways to live together but never experience true freedom. It is only in the light that we are free to grow into our full potential. It is only in Christ that we see the glorious possibility of human life. We are called to experience the possibility of that freedom as our lives are transformed step by step through God's gift to us of the Spirit.

4

When we look at the church it is easy to be discouraged, but it is God who has given us our ministry and God's grace must be sufficient. I will not, therefore, use any tricks or devices to make the gospel more appealing or to draw in some who come for the show and not the substance. Why should we need to embellish God's word with human artifice or conceal it behind the rhythms of the world? It is one thing to sugarcoat a pill which may have a bitter taste but another to camouflage the gospel which must at last confront us with our sins and show us the glory of the eternal God.

If in fact the gospel is concealed, it is concealed from those who hide themselves from it for fear that the undiminished glory of God's light will blind them. The god of this world has blinded them and they would rather perish in the dark than expose their lives to Christ's burning and healing light. In this dark world we would all be blinded by God's full radiant glory but Christ who is the glory of God has shined in our hearts so that we are able to come to the light of the knowledge of God in the face of Jesus Christ.

What we proclaim, therefore, is never ourselves or any human wisdom but only Jesus as Lord and ourselves as your servants for Jesus's sake. We bring this gospel to you in the frailty of human flesh so that you are not deceived into thinking that the power of the message comes from us. There are always some who set out to sell the gospel by wrapping it in all the trappings of Hollywood as if to promote a new movie and draw the fickle crowd of those who are anxious to be part of the latest trend. They have their passing success while we find ourselves with half-empty buildings, halfhearted congregations, and no security for the future. But we cannot despair. Faced with crushing burdens, we make visible in this time and place the sufferings of Christ. Why should we expect or desire cheering multitudes when we remember that such crowds crucified our Savior? How can we make known his suffering if we appear prosperous and secure? So death is at work in us so that life may come to the world, for the same one who raised Jesus from death will raise us also with him and bring us together into his presence.

Do not be discouraged, dear friends; this time of testing is preparing us for a glory beyond all imagination. The things that we see will die and decay but the unseen reality to which we journey will last forever.

5

Earthquake, flood, and fire may sweep away our human cities but we journey toward the heavenly city, the new Jerusalem, the eternal city which exists beyond the limitations of space and time. Within our earthbound cities we live in fear of the uncontrollable and destructive forces of nature and of human greed. We long for the security not to be found in earthly dwellings and long for the day when our present fragile existence may be taken up into the reality that awaits us. God made us with a desire for the life to come and has sent the Spirit into our hearts as evidence of that life. It is that gift of the Spirit that makes us confident in the midst of chaos. The constant news of disasters reminds us that however comfortable we may be in the cities we build for ourselves, our lives there are incomplete and insecure; we live in exile here and in separation from the Lord who loves us. Nonetheless we make it our goal to live for him and to work to understand the human causes of these disasters and do whatever can be done to remove them. We are responsible for much of the world's evil and it is a false religion that would allow human greed to continue unchecked. It is because our eyes are fixed on the kingdom of God that we see most clearly the iniquity of the earthly city and are moved to work with others for its transformation.

We must all come at last to stand before the Lord Christ and be judged for what we have done in this world, whether good or evil. We believe that we are ready to face that judgment but are deeply concerned for those who are not and are ready to do whatever we can to persuade them. It is not the outward appearance of piety that matters but the inward commitment of the heart. It may be that this persuasion seems like insanity to some as we ignore those standards the world accepts and commit ourselves to God but it is for your sake that we do this so that you may point to us as

one who lives not for himself but for Christ who was raised from
death and opens the way of life. If we live in Christ, we become
part of a new world and the old ways are no longer relevant. We
no longer look at life from the human viewpoint but from God's
perspective. From that perspective everything old is gone; only the
new remains! All this is the gift of God who has reunited us with
God in Christ and has given us the task of showing the world what
this new life is like. We are like ambassadors from the kingdom of
life to the kingdom of death proclaiming peace and forgiveness to
a world that is wasting away. Christ became human for us so that
we might be reunited to God in him.

6

Do you remember how the prophet Isaiah said, "At an
acceptable time I have listened to you, and on a day of salvation I
have helped you?"[30] This is that time! This is the day of salvation!
We want nothing to get in the way of our ministry. We have done
whatever we could to reach the world with the gospel message.
We have traveled endlessly and endured every kind of hardship.
We have suffered shipwreck and train wreck and endless delays in
airports; we have been beaten by policemen, attacked by rioters,
imprisoned by godless governments, and driven out by those who
fear the truth. Lacking food and sleep, exhausted by our work, we
have nonetheless responded to adversity by patience and kindness
and holiness; we have spoken the truth, reached out in love, and
relied on God's strength alone.

Sometimes we have been given every honor and sometimes
everyone has condemned us. We have been called liars, but we tell
the truth; we have seemed to be dying, but we are still alive. We
have enriched others though we have never been rich ourselves; we
have never owned anything and yet we possess untold wealth.

We have been completely honest with you Californians because we love you so much. There may be indifference on your side, but certainly not on ours. I beg you to respond to us and not be so entangled with the world around you that you have no time to respond. How can there be any relationship between those of us who belong to Christ and those who are only concerned for their own agendas? How can here be any relationship between believers and unbelievers, between light and darkness, between holiness and Hollywood? What fellowship can there be between the servant of God and the sexual predator? What resemblance is there between the temple of God and the palaces of profit?

You and I are the living temple of God for the Scriptures often speak of God's desire to live among us and make us a holy people. So separate yourselves from everything that interferes with that relationship. Let God be father and mother to each of you so that you may be indeed God's own children.

7

Since God has offered us so much, dear friends, let us come together in a deeper commitment to the holiness of body and spirit that comes to those who stand in awe of God. Some had written to tell me that you had begun to treat God lightly; that although you have built churches on every corner yet you seemed to have made the church an optional extra. Therefore I wrote to you, not condemning you, for I love you and boast about you. You are constantly in my heart and I am prepared to live and die with you. Yet I have to ask you to consider whether your commitment to Christ has really changed your world?

When Timothy visited you he was greatly impressed with what you have accomplished. You have built great cities with marvelous schools and hospitals, museums and galleries. You travel easily from one place to another. Your stores are filled with the produce of the world: exotic fruits and stylish clothes, conveniences beyond the reach of the greatest emperors of past ages. The wisdom of the ages is stored in your libraries and available to you at the touch of a button. Political leaders appeal for your support and offer a society constantly remade to please you. Surely God has given you great gifts, gifts beyond what most human beings have ever known. But surely these are not given to you because you are more admirable and deserving than any other human beings. Others have worked harder, sacrificed more, worshiped more faithfully. Why, then, were you given so much? Was it not in hope that you would act as stewards and share all this with others whose need you know? Was it not in confidence that the instant communications that make you aware of the needs of others would also move you to provide the help they need? But Timothy told me you had become too comfortable and shared too little. It was for that reason that I wrote to you somewhat harshly. I was concerned that you might not understand the love that moved me to write and my hope that, when I come, I might find that you had examined your way of life and begun again to live as you did at first, renouncing all self-concern and striving only to know and serve Christ in others.

If I caused you grief by saying these things, I must tell you it has caused me grief as well. Indeed, I regretted writing as I did because you are my joy and confidence in Christ. But godly grief can lead to repentance and renewal. I trust therefore that Timothy will return in due time to bring me reassurance of your faithfulness so that I may rejoice to hear of all that you have done to renew your obedience to Christ.

8

We want to tell you, dear friends, about the abundance of grace God has granted the churches of Africa, for in spite of conflicts, drought, and persecution, even in great poverty, their abundant joy has overflowed in a zealousness for the gospel and even in making generous gifts to others. I can tell you that they have borne faithful witness and given freely far beyond their means, begging us for the privilege of taking part in the offering we are receiving for those who have lost homes and work in the recent disasters, so that their faith is spoken of everywhere. I will not give you a command but I will suggest that you might measure your own faithfulness against that of theirs. I know what you are able to do; you have done so well in faith and knowledge that we know you will abound also in generosity so that as we have boasted of you to others in the past we will be able to boast of you again.

In all this, we follow, of course, the generous example of the Lord Jesus, who, for love of us, set aside all the riches of the universe to share the poverty of human life in order that he might share with us those riches which we could not hope to earn. So it is appropriate for you to set a higher standard for yourselves and join together in reaching out to others not according to your ability as you might measure it but according to the generosity of God to you. We are all too ready to consider our limitations, but it is God who gives us life and enables us to serve, and God is unlimited. As we learn to rely more fully on God we become able to do more than we have ever imagined.

Remember also that the value of the gift is not measured in shekels or euros or dollars but by the free generosity of the donor. A gift given grudgingly gains no glory for the giver. Our God is one who gives us enough for our needs. In the desert, the children of Israel found manna that was always enough and never too much. So now as well, God has given us enough for our need but not enough for our greed. I have no wish to put pressure on you for then the gift is not free; I hope only that you will consider in prayer how you might best respond to God the giver and to those others who now stand in need. Do not be sure that you will never stand in need yourselves and remember also that you must give an accounting at the last as good stewards of God's gifts.

Do you not see how God calls us to work together in preserving life and renewing creation? There are many who see life only as a field in which all are able to compete for the available resources so that some will win and others will lose. They have no knowledge of a creator nor any sense of sharing life with those others they find around them. But God in the beginning placed our first ancestor in the garden to care for it and the need to care for this created world is greater now than ever. It seems that God expects us to grow in wisdom and understanding so that we will use the tools we create, not only to make our own lives more productive and comfortable, but also to become better stewards, caring ever more wisely for the good earth around us.

9

I don't need to say any more to you about the campaign for funds for African relief because you have already made it clear that you are eager to help. Just the same, I am sending several of my colleagues to you with this letter since personal contact is always so much more effective than mere letters. They will help coordinate the message you proclaim with that which we ourselves proclaim so that there will be no divisions among us as a result of distance or misunderstanding. They have been useful workers wherever they have been and will, I am confident, be able to work with you to promote the gospel and avoid all appearance of division. Welcome them as you would welcome me and show them why it is that I have so often boasted of your love and faithfulness. I want to be sure that whatever is given is given voluntarily and not because you feel that I am compelling you to give. Giving should always be in proportion to the gift, so that those who have the most will give the most and those who have least will not be expected to give as much. It is always the attitude that matters. You will remember, I am sure, what I have said so often: God loves a cheerful giver.

It is God, Scripture reminds us, from whom comes every gift that we are given: the seed we sow, the harvest we reap, and the bread we eat. God makes no distinction between the rich and the poor, the just and the unjust; the same sun shines on all and the same rain falls on all; it is we who seem unable to imitate God in this equality of treatment; some heap up riches while others go hungry. It is therefore our responsibility and privilege to serve as ministers of God and see that God's gifts are distributed fairly to all and especially where there is poverty and hunger.

There is no greater privilege than to be called to this ministry and you who take part in it will be richly blessed, not least by the ties that will be forged between yourselves and your fellow Christians and by their prayers of thanksgiving for your generosity. Thanks be to God for the boundless gifts we are given.

10

There are some among you who cite my letters as their authority in support of some of your political controversies—as if I were concerned for narrow issues of patriotism or transient matters of governmental authority. I will deal with these individuals when I come, but let no one imagine that I will not use my authority to condemn all such dilution and distortion of the gospel. God is able to work through whatever human forms prevail, whether tyranny or democracy, whether power is centralized or dispersed, so long as we seek peace and act justly and the poor are not despised. If you are able to move your government toward justice, you should do so; if not, you must do all you can to serve the needs of your society yourselves. If you protest injustice and suffer for it, you are privileged to share in Christ's sufferings, but anger and impatience must have no place among us. Human anger cannot accomplish God's purpose.

We act within the limitations of human nature and human wisdom but we are not satisfied with the human reasoning that so often divides societies and alienates brothers and sisters within the church. All arguments that rest on proud human reason will be demolished and every human system will be destroyed. Pay careful attention to what I am saying: if you are confident in Christ, do you think I am not a follower of Jesus also? I have no desire to boast, but I have Christ's own commission to build you up in faith and I will not accept the demands of those who claim to be someone important but cannot speak for me. I write this now so that I need not embarrass you when I come; but I will come and I will challenge those who claim any other authority face to face. There are indeed many issues that divide us but let them be resolved with patience and prayer and with good will toward all who seek to serve the Lord Jesus. There are too many who use the gospel to gain power and influence not remembering that Christ sought no such goals but in humility submitted himself to the powers of that day, preferring to suffer rather than to confront power with power. The glory of God is revealed in humility and self-giving love, not in the purchase of influence and in political struggles. I hope I can come to you in the meekness and gentleness of Christ but I will not hesitate to condemn those who prefer another way. It is not those who commend themselves who are approved as God's messengers but those in whom Christ's humility is evident.

11

Will you bear with me now in my foolishness? I had hoped to present you to Christ in marriage and it seems to me you have been beguiled by another suitor, or perhaps that you are easily beguiled by any handsome and eloquent suitor who comes along. It seems as if you listen readily to anyone who claims to speak in Christ's Name even if the Jesus they proclaim is not the one to whom we introduced you. You seem quite willing to accept any spirit or gospel, whatever the latest version of it may be, and to honor any apostles with a gift for self-promotion. Now, I may be unfamiliar with your language but surely you must recognize that we know the gospel far better than these latecomers whose knowledge has more to do with video screens, pop music, and fundraising. Did I commit some sin by humbling myself in order to raise you up or by proclaiming the gospel to you free of charge? When I was with you and had needs, I robbed other churches so that I would not need to ask anything of you. I hope you will forgive me, but I refuse to burden you in any way so that those false apostles who disguise themselves as apostles of Christ and impress you so much will have no opportunity to claim equality with us. Even Satan, you know, disguises himself as an agent of light so it is hardly surprising if his servants also come before you with every appearance of honesty and good will. You can be sure they will be judged for what they do.

Perhaps you think I am a fool not to compete with these new apostles, so let me ask you to bear with me in my foolishness; I cannot refrain from boasting. Since those who impress you boast of their accomplishments, let me boast also. You have let them prey on you and enslave you and take advantage of you or even insult you. It embarrasses me to admit that we have never done such things. But whatever anyone else may boast of—this is foolishness—I will boast of more. Are they apostles? I was one of the first. Are they descendants of Abraham—Jewish, Christian, or Muslim—so am I. Are they ministers of the gospel—this is madness—I am a better one having worked harder and longer in the cause of Christ than any others. I have been flogged and stoned and beaten with rods, in constant danger on land and sea, in storm and shipwreck, attacked both by the open enemies of the gospel and by those who claimed to be its friends. United with the faithful in the body of Christ in every age, I have been tortured by Roman soldiers and by the Inquisition, denounced, arrested, and threatened by supporters and opponents of the Reformation, sent into exile by New England Puritans and Russian communists, driven out by slave holders and by those who hunt down illegal aliens, forced underground by agents of the Japanese emperor and the Chinese People's Republic, mocked and ignored by the comfortable Christians of your American churches. I have been cold and thirsty, hungry and sleepless, attacked by professed friends who proved false, betrayed by those to whom I turned in confidence. Who is weak and I am not weak? Who is mocked for their faith and I am not indignant? If I must boast in my foolishness, I will boast of those things that unite me to Christ in his suffering.

12

Nothing is gained by boasting, but since I have begun, let me continue. I will say something about our spiritual life and tell you about the visions and revelations I have had. Nothing is more dangerous than to speak of such private matters and compare them because these are not given to be shared but only to strengthen us in our personal growth. They are not to be sought for but only to be accepted gratefully if they come. I will tell you, however, that many years ago I was given visions—whether in the body or out of it I cannot tell you—but it seemed that I was caught up into heaven and saw and heard things that cannot be expressed in human words. If I am to boast, I might boast of that experience and I would be speaking the truth but I have not spoken of it before and will not again because it is a private matter and not the gospel. However extraordinary these events may have been and however personally gratifying, it is best not to try to impress others in this way so that they also seek the extraordinary sensation and fail to continue with the ordinary work of the gospel. Life is sustained by bread, not cake; it is the daily bread we are to pray for and the daily bread that God unfailingly provides.

I think it is because I was given this special gift that I have also been physically handicapped. There is always a balance provided so that we will not become proud or think we are specially privileged. I have prayed for strength to overcome my weaknesses but it has been made clear to me that I am to rely on God's strength alone. God's strength is most clearly seen in human weakness. It is in the old, the frail, those challenged daily by their limitations that God's glory is most evident.

So I have been satisfied with the physical ability I have and not asked again for anything more. I can do whatever needs to be done through Christ who strengthens me. It is, in fact, very often true that others are more impressed by the evident power of Christ sustaining us in our weakness than by any ability of our own. So I am well satisfied to be weak if Christ is thereby revealed.

You cannot claim that I burdened you in any way; therefore some say that I won you to faith by deceit. Tell me how! Did I entice you with soft seating or food or music or special effects? You know I did not. What good would it do to win you by showmanship and convenience if the gospel is Christ crucified? Will you be faithful in trials if you have never been tested? The gospel is given to change the world, but there are those who have changed the gospel instead. I have delayed my journey to you because I do not want to come and find you still divided and still led astray and I am sure you do not want me to come in anger and judgment. I want to come and find Christ present among you in simplicity and faithfulness and humble service. Is that what I will find?

13

Tell me this: if you ask a nonbeliever to tell you why he or she is not a Christian, what will they tell you? Will they tell you that they see Christians as men and women who have been changed so profoundly that the love of Christ is evident in all that they do? Will they tell you they are not Christians because they are afraid to venture so radical a change themselves? Or will they tell you that the Christians they see are people obsessed with political issues, narrow minded, self-satisfied, and hypocritical? Will they tell you they are put off by the image of Christianity most often projected in the news and could never become part of a movement that seems to have so little concern for others? Such, you may remember, was the ordinary picture of the so-called righteous people of Jesus's time on earth. It was they who held power, who forced their views on others, and saw themselves as fulfilling God's will for human society in every detail. It was they who insisted that they alone understood God's will—but they are forgotten today except as dreadful examples of self-righteous blindness. I do not ask you to outshout such people or argue with them or to seize power from them. I ask you to follow the way of humble and self-sacrificing love. I ask you to be true followers of Jesus.

Farewell, dear friends. Do what you can to set things in order. Listen to what I have said. Work together; love your neighbors; be at peace with all, and the God of love and peace will be with you. The saints here send you their greetings and assure you of their prayers. The grace of our Lord Jesus Christ, the love of God, and the fellowship of the Holy Spirit be with all of you.

THE LETTER TO TEXAS

(GALATIANS)

Dear Friends in Texas,

I write to you as an apostle with no commission from human authorities but rather from Jesus Christ, who was raised from death by God the Father. I write to you on behalf of the members of God's family who are with me. Together we salute you and pray that grace and peace may be yours from God our Father and Jesus Christ, our risen Lord, who died to set us free from the evils of this wicked age and open to us a way of life and peace and true freedom.

I find it hard to believe that you have turned away so quickly from the gospel I proclaimed to you and are following a different gospel. Of course there is no other gospel, but I think you have been confused by some who have their own agenda. Whoever they are, I condemn them. Even if an angel from heaven brings you a gospel other than the gospel I preach, let that one be condemned. I said it before and I will say it again: if someone teaches a gospel different from the gospel I teach, let that one be condemned!

Let me make it perfectly clear that I am not seeking human approval. I seek to serve God whether human beings are happy about it or not. Do you think I am trying to please someone? I cannot be a servant of Jesus Christ and try to please people. You surely know my background: that I was brought up in the strictest school of Judaism and studied under its greatest teachers for many years in Jerusalem. When I first heard of the church I was shocked and took it upon myself to persecute the church and try to destroy it. God, however, intervened in my life and gave me a specific ministry to the Gentiles so I spent a long time working through the meaning of that commission and only then conferred with the other apostles. Finally, after three years, I did meet with Peter and James and told them what I had been called to do and they made no objection. They asked only that I remember the poor and that

I was eager to do anyway. So if anyone comes from them to tell you something else, they should go back and ask Peter and James themselves. They know our agreement. They have their work to do and I have mine. My work is to proclaim a gospel of freedom and grace that I received through a revelation of Jesus Christ and that is what God sent me to proclaim to you. So why have you been so eager to embrace another gospel and put yourselves in bondage again to the law?

2

Let me give you some examples of what I mean. Throughout your churches you proclaim rightly enough the saving death of Jesus on the cross and you rejoice in being set free from your sins by the blood of Christ. That is good, but then you turn back to the law to condemn others and to enforce patterns of behavior for others saying that their lives must be ruled by law. I am told that you condemn those who live in faithful relationships though many of you have failed to be faithful in your own relationships and have been glad to receive forgiveness and be offered a new beginning. But if you have failed to be faithful yourselves how can you condemn those who are faithful? Why should the law you have broken apply to others if you cannot keep it yourselves?

Are you not also returning to the bondage of law when you deny all access to medical help for those who cannot face the difficulties of childbirth? I myself condemn all those who would prevent life from emerging or restrict the lives of children or shorten the lives of the sick and dying or end any life prematurely. God is the Lord of life and sent the Son to open the way of life. I repeat, God is the Lord of life and we have been given no authority to act on God's behalf to determine when life should begin or end. But when did Jesus ever erect a law by which we might judge others? "Do not judge, so that you may not be judged,"[31] was his teaching, yet you judge others and condemn those who disagree with you. I wish all abortion clinics could be closed this very day, but I cannot force my opinion on others whose circumstances and motives are unknown to me. I pray for them but I will not turn to the law to compel them against their will.

And how, if you value life, can you as followers of Jesus Christ use the law to bring death to those who have taken the lives of others? Did not Jesus, dying under the law, forgive his murderers and open heaven to his fellow sufferer? Can you truly imagine that Jesus would condemn anyone to death? How can we as Christians, condemned by the law ourselves and forgiven in Jesus Christ, condemn others no matter how evil their deeds? Let them be removed from society and allowed an opportunity to understand the evil they have done and repent and find forgiveness but let us not stain our own hands with the blood of others.

Or how can you pass laws to condemn and imprison and remove the stranger among you? Even the law of Moses commanded that, "The alien who resides with you shall be to you as the citizen among you; you shall love the alien as yourself, for you were aliens in the land of Egypt."[32] If you insist on using the law, surely the law should treat all alike. You say, "They have broken the law," but I say that all have broken the law and all can find forgiveness in the Lord. Find ways to live in peace with each other so that the world will see compassion in us and not fearfulness and anger.

We who have come to believe in Jesus Christ seek to be justified by faith in Christ and not by obedience to the law, but if I then turn back to the law and seek to create righteousness by the law, I am building up again that by which I myself was condemned. I died to the law in order to live in Christ and the life I find in him depends on faith in the Son of God who loved me and gave himself for me. We must not nullify the grace of God, for if righteousness comes through the law, then Christ's death becomes meaningless.

3

You foolish Texans! Who has bewitched you? Tell me this: when you received the gospel did you become Christians by obedience to the law? Of course you learned the law but that was to your condemnation. You held up the law to see your failure and found nothing in it to enable you to escape the penalty. When the law comes, we die, but when grace comes we are set free from the law to live in Christ. I have been crucified with Christ; I have died with him in order to live in him and the life I find in him is not lived by the law but by grace.

Before faith came, we were like children who must learn the rules of good behavior and be disciplined when they fail to keep the rules, but now that faith has come we are challenged to behave like adults who have no further need to be guided by rules. The law was our teacher to bring us to Christ, to show us our need for a Savior, but not to leave us still constrained and bound by law and surely not to bind others with the law.

Am I saying that the law is opposed to the promises of God? Not at all! If any law could bring righteousness, the law given to Moses would have done exactly that. That law is good and righteous and holy, but that law brings only death. So also the laws you turn to bring only anger and disobedience and turmoil. The laws you pass, like the law of Moses, serve only to reveal our failure as a society to bring healing and renewal to a sinful world. In our weakness and failure, we turn back to the law, but by grace we are able to bring the light of Christ to shine in the dark places.

Remember that our story begins with the story of Abraham who responded to God in faith and went out not knowing the way ahead of him but trusting that God was able to accomplish God's purpose. So also we who respond in faith must believe that God is able to fulfill the promise to us not by outward obedience to the law but by the inward renewal of the Holy Spirit. We who are baptized have put on Christ and become children of God through faith. Now therefore we have become joined with Christ in whom there is no more distinction of persons; there is no longer Hispanic and Anglo, there is no longer black and white, there is no longer male and female, but all are one in Christ Jesus.

4

Human beings who are not free cannot live without fear of the power of sin and death that enslaves them and all human beings. Those who live in fear tend also to lash out at others, creating a need for laws to restrain us. Therefore the story of God's action in human life is the story of how God has acted to release us from fear and to call the people of God to live in freedom. The celebration of Passover remains a celebration of freedom from slavery in Egypt and the celebration of Easter remains a celebration of freedom from the power of sin and death.

Americans should know very well the meaning and value of freedom; most Americans came to your country in search of freedom from the power of governments that allowed too little opportunity for people to shape their own lives. You have fought two wars on your own territory for freedom, first from a foreign power and second for your own black citizens. You have also fought wars in Europe and Asia to help others win or maintain their freedom.

In the fulness of time, God sent the Son, born of a woman, born under the law, to free those who are under the law and to make you God's children by adoption and grace. It is because you are the children of God that you pray to God as Father; it is because you are the children of God that you are heirs of eternal life and free from the fear of death. But if you have been set free, why would you seek once again to be enslaved and subject yourselves to the tyranny of the law?

You rightly insist on freedom to shape your own life but you have not yet understood and accepted the freedom from sin and fear of death that God gives you in baptism and you therefore lash out against those whose lives are different from yours and who seek the freedom promised not only by the gospel but by your own founding documents. If you seek to limit government's intrusion on your own lives, how can you then use the power of the government to limit the freedom of others? I begin to fear that all I have done to proclaim the gospel to you has been wasted.

What is the value of your churches and schools if you remain in bondage to fear? Why do you send out missionaries to proclaim freedom to others if you yourselves remain in captivity? You are generous to others, both neighbors in need and those in foreign lands, yet you turn in anger on those who differ with you and from you as if you have no knowledge of the power of God or the true meaning of freedom. I am in as much anguish over your behavior as if I were a woman in labor, as if I myself needed to give you a new birth in freedom. I wish I could come to you and we could sort out our differences for I am deeply troubled by what I have heard of your life.

Tell me, you who set such store by the Bible, do you not know the Bible? Have you not read the story of Joseph and his brothers? Do you not remember how innocent Joseph was sold into slavery while his guilty brothers remained free? Yet Joseph, a stranger in a foreign land, in slavery and prison, was able to save his people from starvation, while his brothers, who thought they were free and who once had the power to betray him and persecute him, found themselves dependent on him for their lives. So it has often been that God does not work through those who hold the world's power but through those who are the outcasts and yet know the freedom that is God's gift to those who have faith. This, my friends is our true calling also: we may be enslaved by possessions and insecurity, but we are called to be free.

5

God created you for freedom, and that is the gift Christ gives us. Never give up your freedom or weigh yourselves down with law. If you let yourselves be seduced by the notion that laws can make the world a better place, Christ is useless to you. Once you start down that road, there is no turning back until you have lost your freedom entirely. Laws are necessary, of course, to protect you from dangers and ensure your security, but they cannot make people good. It is through the Spirit, by faith, that we hope to change other lives as ours have been changed. If we are to be a leavening influence on the world around us, it will be accomplished by the evidence of the Spirit in the lives we live.

Let me be very clear: freedom is not an excuse for self-indulgence. The way of the cross is not a smooth road with no challenges or hardships. If it were, why would I still be suffering and encountering such opposition? We are, of course, to discipline our lives and conform them to Christ in every way and use our freedom to become servants of our fellow Christians and all those in need. The whole law is summed up, as you know, in the one commandment, "You shall love your neighbor as yourself."[33] But if you are at war with each other, you will hardly find the peace of Christ in your hearts. If you attempt to constrain others, you will have no freedom yourselves.

Live in the power of the Spirit and pay no attention to the unlimited temptations around you. Your world is constantly offering you ways to waste your time and resources in goods and activities that add nothing of lasting value to your life but do fill up your time and empty out the treasure that might have been used to help heal the world's pain. Should I make a list? The actions of evil are obvious: intemperance, promiscuity, violent words and acts, demeaning others, spreading false rumors, racist language, false advertising, mistreatment of employees, fraud, and other such actions. But the fruit of the Spirit is love, and love produces joy and peace and patience, kindness and generosity and faithfulness, gentleness and self-control. Against these there is no law. Those of us who belong to Christ have learned to crucify and put to death the urge to please ourselves. There is then no more room for conceit and envy. So if we are to live by the Spirit, let the Spirit be our guide.

6

Dear friends, if a member of your congregation is creating dissension, you who are still guided by the Spirit should reach out to them in a spirit of gentleness and seek for reconciliation. Be careful not to create dissension yourselves. Since we all have burdens to bear, let us find ways to help each other, sharing our strengths as well as our weaknesses. Those who think they have it made are fooling themselves. Measure yourself by the standard God holds up to you in Christ and give thanks for what God's grace enables you to accomplish. Share the gifts you are given and especially with those who teach you.

Never imagine that you will be able to escape judgment for your failures. God is not fooled; you will harvest whatever you plant. If you plant thorn trees, you cannot harvest apples. If you seek to

satisfy yourself, you will have only those passing pleasures to show
for it, but if you open yourself to the Spirit, you will receive eternal
life. Let's not get tired of doing the right thing, for we will receive
the gift of life if only we don't give up. So let's work for the good
of others whenever we have the chance, and especially those who
share our life in the church.

Look at the size of the letters I am writing here myself:

it is those who want others to think they are
righteous who call for laws to control the evils in
our society even though they have no intention of
subjecting themselves to any law. All they want is to
boast of their own righteousness. But let me boast of
nothing except the cross of Christ by which the world
has been crucified to me and I have died to the world.
For it is neither laws nor freedom that matters finally
but only new life in Christ. May mercy and peace be
to those who follow this rule and to all the people of
God. From now on, let's have no disagreements; I
suffer enough already for Jesus.

May the grace of our Lord Jesus Christ be with
your spirit, brothers and sisters. Amen.

THE LETTER TO PHILADELPHIA

(PHILIPPIANS)

Dear Friends in Philadelphia,

Timothy and I send greetings to all of you, God's people in Philadelphia, with your clergy and leaders: may you have grace and peace from God our Father and the Lord Jesus Christ. I am always grateful to God when I think about you. My prayers are filled with joy because of the way you have been serving God from the first settlement of your community to the present time and I am confident that you will continue to find ways to serve until you complete the mission God has given you. The very name of your city reflects the commitment to peace and unity which is central to the Gospel message and that you have always recognized and honored. It was an ancestor of yours who painted his vision of the peaceable kingdom and reminded all of us that enmity between nations is unacceptable to God and that we must live by that vision, not what some would call "the real world." We seek no human kingdom but rather God's reign of peace in which the prophet tells us that "nation shall not lift up sword against nation, neither shall they learn war anymore."[34]

I long to visit you as soon as possible but meanwhile I continue to pray that you will grow in understanding and insight so that you can determine how best to serve and work for the day we await, the day when God's justice and peace will prevail. Meanwhile it is important that you play your full part in working toward that day so that you will have nothing to regret when it comes.

I want you to know, dear friends, that all my own difficulties have simply helped to spread the gospel. Those who oppose me have attracted attention and made people ask what the issue may be with the result that the good news of Jesus has become even better known. There are some who proclaim the gospel simply to get attention for themselves and others who do it for God's glory; either way attention is drawn to the message. The publicity is good from that perspective, but the controversy divides us so that the world hears of the gospel but not of a message of love and unity.

I hope I will continue to have opportunities to bear witness and that I will be able to do it in such a way that Christ will be lifted up and honored. I hope that you agree with me that life itself is of no value unless we use it to God's glory. If I am in this world, I can serve the Lord and if I die, I will be with the Lord, so that is a hard choice to make. I would happily die now in order to be with Jesus except that I believe I can still serve God in human flesh. That being the case, I will do all that I can to support you in your witness and ministry so that you will continue to grow in faith and joy. So live your lives in a way that brings glory to God, working side by side with a common mind, and never allow yourselves to be frightened into silence by those who sneer at you. You can be sure that God is able to use all your difficulties for your own benefit and that of others also. Even if you suffer, it is no loss because God can use your suffering to strengthen your faith and make a witness to others. It is through God's gift that we have come to believe and God will enable us also to endure and to grow whatever opposition we may encounter.

2

If I can say anything now to encourage you, to comfort you, to share the Spirit's power with you, and to express my compassion and sympathy, I would only ask you in return to make my joy complete by becoming a community of peacefulness and unity in which no one acts from ambition or pride, but in which each of you seeks first to serve others and in which each of you thinks of others as better than one's self.

Remember the hymn we sing that reminds us of what is central to our faith:

At the Name of Jesus every knee shall bow,
every tongue confess him king of glory now;
'Tis the Father's pleasure we should call him Lord
who from the beginning was the mighty Word.

Humbled for a season to receive a name
from the ranks of sinners unto whom he came,
faithfully he bore it, spotless to the last,
brought it back victorious when from life he passed;

Bore it up triumphant with its human light
through all ranks of creatures, to the central height,
to the throne of Godhead, to the Father's breast,
filled it with the glory of that perfect rest.[35]

That, my dear friends, is the challenge before us: to respond to that same God who came so humbly in Jesus and to make room for the Spirit to work within us in fear and trembling. The Spirit inspires us to humble ourselves in the same way that Jesus did, seeking nothing for ourselves but always the good of others. Whoever is poor, whoever is powerless, it is to them that Jesus came and in them that God is present. You are not called to control the lives of others or even your own life but to live with the simplicity of children unconcerned with the prestige and power that those around you care about.

Bear faithful witness always for peace as your ancestors and founders did. The gospel was first proclaimed in a world apparently at peace, but that was not a real peace because it was based on the power of the Roman armies. There was no war, but also there was no peace in human hearts. What seemed like peace was only fear of Rome. Peace is not simply an absence of war; true peace is found only in freedom, in lives that are governed by the Spirit and filled with the joy and peace that only the Spirit can bring.

Would you work for peace? Work, then, to change human hearts, to change them from the endless and useless search for wealth and power to a fruitful search for the welfare of others. Nations can never make peace; peace begins in the human heart and spreads out to transform society as the yeast transforms the lump. The Lord taught his disciples to love their enemies and do good to those who are filled with hatred; that's what you need to do and, when you do, the Spirit will strengthen you. The first fruit of the Spirit is love; love has the power to break down walls and overcome enmity. Continue to give yourselves to this work.

As soon as possible I will send Timothy to you so that he may see for himself how you are and tell you about my life. I have all too few fellow workers like him, men and women who devote themselves completely to the work of the gospel. I will also send Edward back to you. He has served me faithfully but he was concerned because you had heard that he was ill—indeed, he was and near death—but he has recovered and would like to thank you for your concern and join with you once again in your work for the gospel and for peace.

3

I may be repeating myself, but it is easy for me to write and good for you to be reminded of basics. Rejoice in the Lord. Beware of cynics and skeptics. Beware of those who claim to be Christian but create division and disturb the peace of the community. If anyone has a claim to the title of Christian, I have more: I was called in a vision by the Lord himself; I have been beaten and imprisoned, and I have journeyed constantly to carry the gospel to distant places. If they boast of the Bible, I can claim that I have written many of the pages of that book myself. Yet whatever claims I might make, I will regard everything as worthless for the sake of the overwhelming joy of knowing Jesus Christ as my Lord and Savior. For his sake I have lost or given away every possession and claim to prominence and hold it to be so much worthless trash so that I may gain Christ and live in him alone. All I ask is the opportunity to share Christ's suffering and death so that I may know him and the power of his resurrection. Even now I do not claim to have reached the goal but I continue to do all I can to win that race and be given the crown of victory at the end of the day. I trust, dear friends, that you also will exert yourselves to reach the goal and be awarded the prize: God's call to share eternal life with our risen Lord. Hold fast what you have achieved.

Imitate me, my friends, and pay attention to those who lead holy lives in this world. There are many who like to sound religious but have no other purpose than to fill their own bank account. Their god is worldly wealth and their glory is this world's fame. I have told you of them before and tell you of them again with tears: their desire is for earthly things and they show their loyalty to their nation by deriding and attacking others. But our citizenship is not in this world and our final values do not involve patriotic symbols. God's peace is greater than earthly peace but those who seek it will make peace now in their community. We seek the welfare of our community by promoting peace with others and never accepting borders and boundaries that divide us from our fellow Christians and others of God's children by whatever name they are called. A city of brotherly love must seek to create a nation of brotherly love and to find a world of human love transformed by God's love until all hatred and self-seeking is swallowed up in the search for God.

4

I love you and long to be with you, my brothers and sisters. Your existence as a Christian community is my great joy and satisfaction. Stand fast in the Lord. If there are any among you who are involved in disagreements, urge them to remember what unites them. You are all my companions in the faith and have worked with me to spread the gospel. Your names are written in the Book of Life, so there must be no divisions among you. There is nothing that can divide us that is more important than what unites us.

As I said before, so I will say again: Always rejoice in the Lord. Let me repeat it: Rejoice. Think how near to us our Savior is and let your lives be transformed by his presence. Be gentle; be confident; turn to God in prayer with all your requests and your thankfulness. As you learn to live in peace, your example will make a difference in the community, and God's own peace, beyond anything we can understand, will fill your hearts and minds.

In a world of chaos and confusion, a world in which the media fill your homes with every sort of useless foolishness, you will find it helpful to center your thoughts on those aspects of life where God's Spirit can be seen at work. Think about those who provide faithful leadership in your community and those who give themselves to the care of those in need; fill your thoughts with the words of Scripture and prayer and hymns. Try to follow the example I have given you and you will find your life filled with God's peace.

In closing, let me thank you for your renewed support for those who share my ministry and who are carrying the gospel to new areas of the world. It is easy to forget those in distant places but hard for them to carry on their ministry without your support. In the early days of your history you gave generously to those who ministered to Native Americans and in later years you worked hard to free those of African descent. Now there is enormous need in such distant places as eastern Africa where war and drought have left millions dependent on the generosity of others. God has given you great gifts and you have always shared them freely, yet now, more than ever, I ask you to be aware of the needs of those you do not see. I myself have sometimes had plenty and sometimes very little but I have learned to go on my way whether with much or with little relying always first of all on God who strengthens me. I have been repaid in full and given more than enough. So, also, God will provide for you richly as you provide for others.

Some concern themselves with the threat of scarcity; others rely on God's abundance. I am confident that God, who provides abundantly for us and has opened to us all the riches of God's glory in Jesus Christ our Lord will meet your every need. To our God and Creator be glory now and forever in Christ Jesus. Greet your fellow Christians. Those who are with me send you their greetings. May the grace of the Lord Jesus Christ guide and strengthen all of you. Amen.

THE LETTER TO COLORADO

(COLOSSIANS)

Dear Christian Friends in Colorado,

My companions and I send you greetings: may God's grace and peace be with you.

Although I have not had the privilege of visiting you and your beautiful state, I have often heard of your faith in Christ Jesus and of the love you have shown toward your fellow Christians because of the hope that is held out for us in the coming world. You know of this hope because you are fortunate to stand in a long tradition of faithful witnesses and have worked to bear your own witness and share your faith with others so that the fruit of that faith is visible not only in your community but throughout the world. Ever since we heard of this we have offered praise to God for you and prayed that your community would continue to grow and flourish in the faith just as others are doing wherever the gospel is preached.

We praise God for your faithfulness and we have offered our prayers and thanksgiving for you constantly since first we heard news of you, asking that you really learn what God's will for you is and that you lead the kind of lives that Christ taught and that will be pleasing to him. You will need strength to do that and you will be called to endure hard times. I pray that you will be given strength and patience to become true witnesses to the power of love. In the midst of conflict and suffering you will find the glorious power of God at work within you and you will find that you are able to bear witness to the one who has rescued us from the power of darkness and transferred us into the realm of light as members of Jesus' body. It is in him that we are rescued from the need to be popular and successful in this world, and forgiven for our failures, and raised to a new and eternal life.

Christ Jesus is a savior and redeemer whose true nature is not understood even by many who proclaim him; they worship a smaller god whose interests are limited to the politics of the day and the promise that we will feel better. But the God we worship is one whose reality so far surpasses our own that no words can express it and no human minds can take it in. Look down from space and your soaring mountains are barely visible. Look up from your mountains and God is visible everywhere, and invisibly present in the farthest galaxies, present in all things and beyond all things, and present among us in Christ Jesus in whom that known and unknown God became visible in human flesh. Through him the vast and infinite universe came into being and in him space and time are held together. The church is his body and we are its members, for Christ dwells in each of us and draws us together to share his life. It is God's purpose to unite all things in him, bringing together the varied elements of the human family and reconciling all that are divided, making peace through the blood of the cross.

You live in a society that uniquely reflects God's purpose, for all the races and tribes of humanity are represented among you and have been able to accept a common though lesser vision of the unity to which we are called. Insofar as your society holds together it provides a foretaste of the kingdom and insofar as it is divided it gives us evidence of the continuing power of sin. But all the divisions that create anger and fear and hostility and that impoverish human society must be overcome in Christ Jesus so that you are able to appear before God's throne in the beauty of holiness, freed from the darkness of past deeds and raised in him to a new and eternal life.

My mission is to make this gospel known and to reveal the mystery, God's hidden purpose, which is now made plain in Jesus: to unite and transform all men and women so that they can grow into their full potential and offer themselves to God in thankfulness.

2

I want you to know how hard I am working to make this gospel known to you and your neighboring communities so that they and you will be encouraged and united in love and have a full understanding of the rich treasure which God pours out on us. I may not be physically present with you but I am certainly with you in spirit and gratified to see the strength of your faith. See to it that no one draws you away from this gospel since the universe itself depends on our perseverance.

Although God in Christ brought the universe into being for our sake, it was not until the present age that human beings have been able to play so transformative a part in the universe, but as we see the changes in the climate that are consequences of our failures in stewardship we must come to realize that we have the power as well to restore and renew our earthly environment. Efforts now to conserve the physical environment and the rich tapestry of animal life begin to fulfill God's command to the first humans to take dominion over all the earth and to use that dominion no longer selfishly but for the benefit of the whole. In the same way, we see today the constant extension of the span of human life and therefore an expanded opportunity to serve the human community, to bring wars to an end, to provide adequate education and health care for all, and root out injustice of every kind. Truly you live in a critical time when human beings can choose to create or destroy and must come together in faith to exercise the stewardship you are given of the enormous resources of the creation for the benefit of all.

All this begins, of course, with your response of faith with thanksgiving and praise: that your lives be rooted and grounded in Christ and nourished by him as plants are nourished by the sun and soil. Make sure that no one draws you away to any lesser understanding of the faith, to a faith that is controlled by rules and laws (don't do this and don't do that) or one that is purely an emotional response controlled by our feelings rather than our minds and lacking in depth and insight. Some rules can be useful and our emotions are a great gift but to grow into the full stature of Christ is more than these.

There was a time when all of us were separated from God and seeking only to satisfy ourselves, working to gain at the expense of others and fearful that others might take away what we had gained. Truly we were dead in our sins, but we were baptized and died to that self-centered and sinful life in order to be raised with Christ through faith in the power of God. In him the legal demands of past ages were taken up and nailed to the cross so that we might be set free from the burden of sin and enabled to live to the glory of God.

3

So if, in fact, you have been raised with Christ, make it your purpose to live a transformed life in which Christ's will is done here as perfectly as it is done in heaven. When you commit yourself to Christ, you die to this world and your real life is in Christ in God. Examine yourselves from that point of view and ask whether each aspect of your life is compatible with a risen life. Does your sexual life reflect God's faithfulness? Do you manage your possessions in a way that reflects God's generosity? Do you control your emotions in a way that reflects the constancy of God's love? Does your speech reflect the truthfulness of the word God speaks to us in the gospel and in the life of Jesus Christ?

To live the new life in Christ is like taking off our old apparel and putting on a new garment; it is like enlisting in a training program, like enrolling in a course of study, like setting out to renew and remodel ourselves in the image of Christ, the image of God from which we have fallen away. In this renewed life, the divisions that plague our human societies disappear and the labels of white and black, Hispanic and Anglo, gay and straight, immigrant and native become irrelevant because Christ is all and in all. You are those God has chosen, God's beloved, called to live lives that reflect God's holiness. Human anger and impatience and greed and jealousy must be replaced by kindness and patience and humility and concern for others. Always be ready to forgive. These same qualities must be characteristic of your society so that your first concern is for others, especially the sick and handicapped and needy. Choose leaders also in whom these qualities are evident, who speak truthfully and never tolerate slander or dishonesty. Make love and peace your first priority so that the body of the church is united and able to act effectively to make Christ known.

Make the reading of Scripture a daily practice so that the Word of God can work productively in your life and enable you to teach others and grow in wisdom. Be thankful and express your gratitude in hymns and songs of praise. Whatever you do and whatever you say, let it be in the name of Jesus to whom and through whom we offer our prayers and praise.

Let your family life and other relationships reflect your faith and not the behavior of others around you. Let those who are married honor their partners, seeking to serve and not control. Let parents set an example for their children, encouraging them and supporting them as they grow in physical and mental ability and especially in faith, providing guidance while respecting their individuality. In your work, be respectful of others whether they are your employers or employees, and perform your work as an offering to your Lord knowing it is God who enables you to work and that your final responsibility is to the Lord Christ who judges all people impartially.

4

Those of you who are employers have a special responsibility toward those you employ. You are, of course, concerned with the bottom line and must earn enough to balance your books, but when you employ someone you gain the power to shape another human being's life for good or ill. You depend on them to do their work reliably and well but they depend on you for life itself; indeed, you gain the ability to influence their eternal welfare for if you conduct your relationships in a way that reflects your faith you may be able to draw them to share your faith or strengthen their faith. Be fair and generous in paying them for what they do. Be honest in your dealings with your suppliers; set fair prices for your product; be careful for the environment; be a good steward of all that God has created.

Set aside regular times of prayer and be alert in your prayer, responsive both to the needs of others and to God's will for you. Continue also to pray for us that God will open doors ahead of us as we carry the gospel to new areas and enable us to proclaim the mystery of our faith, the hidden purposes of God in Christ Jesus, that I may make clear the will of God for our salvation. Be thoughtful and careful yourselves in your dealing with those who are not part of the faithful community, using your relationships with such to make a favorable impression. There are too many who call themselves Christians whose speech and manner of life turn many away.

I have many companions here whose names you know who send you their greetings; some are of Gentile families and some even of Jewish and Moslem background; they are working hard for the coming realm of righteousness and have been a great support to me. You can be assured of their constant prayers for you, that God will enable you to stand firm and come to maturity in your conduct.

Make sure you complete the tasks assigned. When you have read this letter send a copy of it to the church in Wyoming and see that you read the letter I sent to them. As you can see, I, Paul, have written these last few words in my own hand. Remember to pray for me. Grace be with you always.

THE FIRST LETTER TO FLORIDA

(I THESSALONIANS)

Dear Friends in Florida,

This letter comes to you, the church of God in Florida, from Paul, Silvio, and Timothy. We wish you grace and peace from God our Creator and Jesus our Redeemer. We always give thanks for all of you and keep you in our prayers because we have seen how hard you work to build up the church and how consistently you place your hope in our Lord Jesus. We know God has chosen you and is at work among you because we see not just your words but the work you do to witness to the gospel and we see how the Holy Spirit strengthens you and gives you such conviction of the truth of the gospel that in spite of all the difficulties placed in your way you are filled with joy and are an example to others all over the eastern part of your country.

You know what kind of life we lived for your sake when we were with you, constantly showing you a way of life different from that of the general population, and you have made yourselves different so that your faith is well known and we have no need to talk about it. Everywhere people talk about the way you welcomed us and turned away from mere pleasure seeking to serve the true and living God and to look for Jesus, whom God raised from the dead, to come into your lives with such power that you would have no fear of the future even when the economy is in frightening condition and powerful storms continue to create destruction.

2

You know, of course, how on our first visit to you we determined that we would let nothing stand in the way of our proclamation of the gospel. We never flattered you or deceived you or made any effort to gain your praise. You know perfectly well that we set out only to please God who had entrusted us with the gospel message and to give you that message in all its purity. We might have set out to impress you with popular music and emotional appeals; we might have thundered warnings of judgment to frighten you. But our hope was to show you instead the love that God has revealed to us in Jesus and to care for you as he cared for those he met, especially those rejected by their society and scorned as sinners. In the same way, I made no demands on you but earned my own living, working night and day so I would be no burden to you. It was always my intention to deal with you as a father and mother care for their children because you were so dear to us. As you know, I set out to show you by my own example the way of life to which God has called us, to live for others and not for our own pleasure or benefit.

You have seen, of course, how we were scorned and rejected and you yourselves have experienced the same treatment from those who would turn the gospel to their own purpose and who entice the ignorant with promises of emotional and financial well-being. On every side, you see new church buildings are erected and programs cleverly devised to make the multitudes feel good about themselves. They glory in numbers and outward show; they provide comfortable seating and easy listening. But I warn you now as I warned you before that the gospel of God is not simply comfort and reassurance but death and new life for those who give themselves to our Lord with no thought of self. This was the message you received from us and that you accepted with joy and faithfulness. This is why we have been so anxious to see you again face to face and why we have felt like orphans in this time of separation. I, Paul, have yearned to see you again and again, but we will come to you soon and we will be overjoyed to see you because when the Lord Jesus comes we will point to you as the fruit of our ministry. Yes, you are the glory and crown of which we boast.

3

This is why we had to know how you are doing and so we decided to stay alone where we are and send Timothy to you so that he could strengthen you in your faith and bring us a report as to your progress. We knew there would be difficult times when all around you others would fall away into an echo-faith, a distorted image of the gospel, and proclaim Christ out of greed and self-seeking and draw many others with them into a broad way that leads to destruction. You will remember how we warned you that some would seek to draw you away from the gospel we proclaimed and tempt you to seek the false security of an easy way, and so it turned out as you now know.

This was the reason why, when I could stand it no longer, I sent Timothy to you to find out whether you had persisted in your faith or whether you had been tempted to follow the crowd and forsake my teaching so that all our labor had been in vain. But Timothy has just returned with the good news that you have resisted temptation and continue to stand firm in the Lord. He told us that you remember us with kind affection and that you continue to pray for us and hope to see us again—just as we long to see you as soon as possible. There is no way we can thank God enough that you stand firm in the faith and fill us with joy before God. Night and day we pray with all our strength that we may see you face to face and help build you up to an even stronger faith. May God our Father and the Lord Jesus direct our way to you and may the Lord enable you to grow in love for each other and for all God's people just as we are filled with love for you. And may God

so strengthen you in holiness of life that God will find you to be
faithful still at the coming of our Lord Jesus with all the saints.

4

Let me only add a few more things: do try to continue making
progress in everything we taught you (as I know you are doing
already) so that your lives will be ever more pleasing to God. You
will remember the instruction we gave you through the Lord Jesus:
God's will for us is our sanctification, the transformation of our
lives. A life of holiness begins with the control of our bodies. We
cannot yield to every bodily urge or impulse as so many of those
around us do. There are many who think that sexual satisfaction is
the purpose of life and who even seek medical help if their sexual
urges are weak, but you know better than that. God created us
for holiness, for lives offered to God and to our neighbors in self-
sacrificing love rather than self-seeking and passing pleasures. We
are never to take advantage of another in any way but to seek their
own welfare before our own. Anyone rejecting this advice is not
rejecting human authority but the will of that same God who has
sent the Holy Spirit into our lives.

Concerning your relationships with each other, you need no
advice from me. God has filled your hearts with love for each other
and not only in your local community but far beyond so that you
reach out to strengthen each other. We would only urge you to
continue to grow in this respect: to live simply, to avoid conflict,
and to rely as much as possible on your own resources. The world
around you tries always to create desires for things we have no need
of. Be satisfied with the material things you have and remember
that they cannot compare in value with spiritual gifts.

We want you to understand also what happens when we die so
that you will not be overwhelmed with grief as many others are.

Our faith begins with the fact that Jesus died and rose again from death, so we can be sure that those who have died will live again through faith in Jesus. We tell you this as God's own word: we will be reunited with those who have died. In earlier days we expected the second coming of Jesus at any moment, but even if it is delayed no one should imagine that this present world will last forever. We may, of course, destroy it ourselves, but whether we do or not, the final trumpet might sound at any time and each moment should be lived with the awareness that this life is not eternal and all that we do will be judged. God calls us and comes to us to gather us into an eternal life with all those we love. Strengthen and encourage each other by reminding them of this.

5

Some things we hardly need to tell you. There are always some who devote their time and energy to predicting the end of the world. Don't waste your time on that. You know perfectly well that life-changing events can seldom be predicted. There are often signs in advance of such catastrophic events as the fall of a dictator, the destructive coming of a hurricane, or the onset of terminal illness but we can never adequately prepare ourselves for them or do much to turn them aside. But you, dear friends, should not be surprised to discover that life in this world is always limited and uncertain. Of course it is, but your life is not dependent on temporal things. You live in the light of Christ, not the light generated by human ingenuity and dependent on a fragile transmission network. Your neighbors may talk about renewable energy and such concern is appropriate, but you also know that no energy source in this world can be renewed forever and that the strength we need for life here and hereafter comes from God alone.

Let us also not be dominated by the latest headlines. Others will buy or sell, party or panic, because their lives are controlled by passing fears and pleasures and worldly worries. But you belong to the Lord and need have no concern for the issues that often dominate your neighbors' lives. God did not create us simply to live out the short span of human life and pass away but to obtain eternal life through our Savior Jesus Christ so that both now and hereafter we will live with him. Therefore continue to help each other and build each other up as you have been doing.

My brothers and sisters, I ask you to remember that those who serve as your pastors have great demands made on them and need your support. They need to challenge you to grow in faithfulness and you must understand that they seek your eternal welfare. So give them the support they deserve. Notice also those in your congregation who are not contributing and try to find ways to involve them in your ministry. Help those who face special challenges at home or at work and be patient with all those who seem discouraged. Never respond to negative conduct with anger or abuse but find ways to do good even to those who seem least deserving of your love.

Let your joy be evident. Keep up your prayers. Be thankful for every new day and use it to God's glory. That is what God asks of us. Be alert and responsive to the guidance of the Spirit. Pay attention to those who write books of spiritual guidance and look for whatever is useful in what they say but test it by the words of Scripture and the wisdom of the great leaders of past times. Never let your behavior bring discredit on the fellowship.

I pray that the God of peace will fill your hearts and minds and keep you strong in faith until the Lord Jesus Christ comes. He has called you to belong to him and he will support you faithfully on your journey. Pray for us. Share the peace with your brothers and sisters. Make sure this letter is passed on to your fellow Christians. The grace of our Lord Jesus Christ be with all of you.

THE SECOND LETTER TO FLORIDA

(II THESSALONIANS)

Dear Friends in Florida,

Silvio and Timothy join me in sending greetings to you, the church of God in Florida, and praying that you may have grace and peace through your faith in God our Creator and the Lord Jesus Christ. It is wonderful to hear of the growth of your faith and the increase of your love for each other. We give thanks to hear this and we are proud to tell others of the way you have only been strengthened by the hardships you have faced in the recent terrible storms that have swept through your state. You have been often in our prayers and we know that when God comes in judgment, your deepened faith will serve you well.

Living, as you do, with an aging population and a vulnerability to extreme weather, it is not surprising that some should concentrate on the end times rather than the present world. No one should doubt that the Lord Jesus will return in that day and strike terror in the hearts of those who have rejected the gospel and lived selfishly without regard for their neighbors or those living in poverty while those who have been faithful will rejoice. Some will say that we should concern ourselves only with preparing for that day but the best preparation is faithful living in the present time, serving those in need and working for peace and justice in your community and throughout the world.

I pray constantly that the Lord will find you worthy of his call and will strengthen you with his grace to keep your baptismal commitment so that the name of our Lord Jesus will be honored by those who know you and many others will be drawn to your community.

2

Let me say more about the obsession with the end times that seems to afflict so many. I beg you not to be shaken by the predictions that are so often made and that remain so often unfulfilled. The Lord Jesus himself said that many would come claiming to know these things and might deceive even the chosen. The powers of evil constantly reassert themselves and claim to possess the truth but their truth is deception and they are never able to gain control, indeed they are destroyed by their own selfishness. Nevertheless, good people are often deceived and follow after these false prophets and false gods, honoring them and contributing to their causes. Many of them even claim the name of Christ and deceive the simple, but you will know them by their fruit. Those who seek power in a way that destroys the peace of the community, that sets neighbor against neighbor, that vilifies others do so because they are dominated by fear rather than faith. But we live by faith and have no fear of a future that belongs always to God.

Do you not remember how I wrote of these things long ago and begged the churches to be confident in spite of all the apparent victories of evil? There were many who feared the triumph of fascism and of communism and sought to terrify their neighbors with baseless speculations, who sought for enemies within and turned friend against friend in a needless search for enemies where there were none to be found; indeed, there were great evils abroad but they were overcome by those who remained steadfast, confident that our God was able to sustain the righteous cause without a need to seek out adversaries even among our friends. Evil at last is self-destructive and cannot withstand the determined resistance of those who love God and seek out first the evil in themselves which is overcome by repentance and God's abundant forgiveness.

I give thanks that God has chosen you to be witnesses to love in the midst of anger and to faith where there is fear and insecurity. Stand firm, brothers and sisters beloved, and continue to serve as you have done in the past so that your community remains unshaken by the fears of others and firm in allegiance to the Lord

Jesus Christ. May our Lord himself who made known to us the love of God and who gives us eternal hope and strength in the gospel, build you up in the truth and enable you to continue in every good work and the word of renewal.

3

Finally, my dear friends, pray for us so that the gospel message may continue to spread and be held in honor everywhere just as it is among you. Pray that we may be rescued from those who would distort the truth and seek to use it for their own ends and their own profit, for not everyone who claims to be faithful is true. I am confident, however, that the Lord will guide and strengthen you to continue doing the work we have given you to do. I pray that the love of God and the strength of Christ will fill your hearts.

Do not associate with those who live in idleness, consumed with curiosity about the rich and famous whose lives may draw the attention of the media but should not interest us, for they are concerned only to indulge themselves and to live without regard for their neighbor's need; they worship their bodies and devote themselves to luxuries rather than seeking to use their gifts to honor the God who made them or the Lord who redeemed them. You will remember, of course, the different example we set you in working to support ourselves and always paying for whatever we needed so that we would never be a burden to anyone.

It is a great tragedy of the present day that many in your society seek for work and cannot find it. You must provide for their needs and seek to create opportunities for them to use their energy and skill in productive ways and for the good of all. Those who cannot work must still eat. We are adopting false values when we honor those who live in luxurious idleness while criticizing others who are idle through no choice of their own.

Never be weary, dear friends, of living lives that are honest and constructive; do not be distracted by those who hold false values and do not think of them as enemies, but show them a better way by the faithfulness of your own conduct.

May the Lord of peace give you peace and strengthen you constantly in all that you do. The Lord be with all of you. I, Paul, wrote this letter myself and you will recognize it as my own writing. The grace of the Lord Jesus be with you.

THE LETTER TO PHILIP LEAMAN

(PHILEMON)

My dear Philip,

My warmest greetings to you and your fellow Christians; may grace and peace be yours from the Lord God our Creator and Jesus our Savior. I give thanks to God often for you in my prayers because I hear so frequently of your faithful witness and the support you give to your fellow Christians. It warms my heart and gives me great joy and encouragement to hear of the way you bear witness to Jesus and make known the love of God in actions as well as words. It gives me special joy to hear of your courage in welcoming into your community those Christians from south of your border who come to you lacking documents but seeking ways to support themselves and their families when they can no longer do so in their own homeland. It is, after all, no choice of theirs but rather the policies of your government that have deprived them of the ability to earn a living where they were so it is hard to see why government policy would then restrict them and prevent them from seeking work where it is available. Some, I am sure, will question your right to reach out to the stranger in your midst but I would ask, "Does God's love for us have borders or limits of any kind? God forbid!" How then can our love for others be restricted or denied by human laws or limits? Scripture, in fact, commands us to welcome the stranger and foreigner and reminds us that our ancestors were foreigners in the land of Egypt, but God brought them out with a mighty hand and nourished and cared for them in the desert they needed to cross and drove out those who did not welcome them in the new land they entered.

I give thanks to God that you have taken leadership in this struggle without waiting for me to ask; such is the evidence that the Spirit of the Lord Jesus, who went first to the poor and outcast, is at work also in you so that you need not be asked to respond to the need that is so evident in every place. Should any question you,

you may assure them that you have my complete support and that I hope to visit you and work with you at the earliest opportunity. I have been imprisoned, as you know, for my own witness to the faith, and others may need to go to prison also for the sake of our labors in the gospel but we cannot be turned aside by those who put human law before God's command. We have, after all, been given a greater freedom that no human power can take away.

Those imprisoned with me send you greetings. Do be ready, however, to receive me for I intend to visit you when I am free to do so. May the grace of the Lord Jesus Christ be with your spirit.

ENDNOTES

1 St. John 10:2

2 Acts 10:34–35

3 Psalm 44:22

4 Zechariah 8:23

5 Isaiah 56:7

6 Psalm 113:3

7 Malachi 2:10

8 Isaiah 2:2-3

9 Isaiah 2:4

10 Isaiah 30:15

11 Isaiah 30:18

12 Deuteronomy 32:21

13 Isaiah 65:1

14 Isaiah 65:2

15 Isaiah 28:16 (But Paul is quoting the Greek Old Testament.)

16 Joel 2:32

17 Psalm 72:11

18 Isaiah 45:23

19 Isaiah 40:13

20 Proverbs 15:1

21 Isaiah 53:3–4

22 Psalm 22:27

23 Psalm 103:13

24 Isaiah 41:5

25 Isaiah 42:6

26 Isaiah 66:19

27 Isaiah 55:8

28 Zechariah 4:6

29 Deuteronomy 16:14
30 Isaiah 49:8
31 Matthew 7:1
32 Leviticus 19:34
33 Leviticus 19:18
34 Isaiah 2:4
35 Paraphrase of Philippians 2:9–11 by Caroline Maria Noel (1817–1877)